Working with spreadsheets

Tutorial

Wendy Yates

Published by Osborne Books Limited
Unit 1B Everoak Estate
Bromyard Road, Worcester WR2 5HP
Tel 01905 748071
Email books@osbornebooks.co.uk
Website www.osbornebooks.co.uk

Design by Laura Ingham

Printed by CPI Group (UK) Limited, Croydon, CR0 4YY, on environmentally friendly, acid-free paper from managed forests.

MIX
Paper from
responsible sources
FSC® C013604

British Library Cataloguing in Publication Data
A catalogue record for this book is available from the British Library

ISBN 978 1909 173 224

Contents of this book

Quick guide to the contents of this book

List of practice exercises

Notes for tutors

Acknowledgements

The author wishes to thank Jon Moore, Bee Pugh and Cathy Turner for their help with the reading, production and design of the text. Special thanks are due to Ian Yates for his technical reading of the text and checking of the exercises and also to Laura Ingham for the designs used in this book. Thanks are also due to Microsoft UK for their kind permission to use screen images from Excel software within the text and to the Association of Accounting Technicians for permission to reproduce sample assessment material.

Author

Wendy Yates has a degree in Pure Mathematics and more than thirty years programming experience, ranging from sophisticated CAD through to business systems.

Wendy has developed a variety of business models, creating comprehensive Excel Macros to automate procedures. Her most recent projects have been to develop Cashflow and Bookkeeping systems in partnership with a major accountancy firm.

Wendy has wide and varied experience of teaching IT in schools, including spreadsheets and CLAIT, and she has also delivered IT courses at South Worcestershire College.

Contents – a quick guide

This section explains at a glance the main contents of each of the seven chapters in this book.

1   Spreadsheet basics

This chapter covers the following basic principles and techniques:

- Useful tips
- Basic spreadsheet structure
- Opening and saving workbooks
- Worksheets
- Enter data into cells
- Copy cells
- Rows and columns
- Change the height of a row or width of a column
- Using basic formulas

2   Formatting the spreadsheet data

This chapter covers the formatting of a spreadsheet:

- Formatting - style
- Formatting - fonts and size
- Number formats
- Cell alignment
- Date format
- Printing and page setup

3   Advanced formatting

This chapter covers more advanced formatting and improving spreadsheet presentation:

- Cell display - borders (border colours and thickness), fill colours
- Move row or column
- Hide row or column
- Conditional formatting
- Cell and sheet protection
- Data validation

4   Spreadsheet functions

This chapter explains the use of built-in functions which are found in most common spreadsheet software packages:

- Formulas
- Functions
- Ranges

- Mathematical functions
- Cell addressing
- Date functions
- Brackets
- IF statements
- Lookup (Vlookup, Hlookup)
- Circular references in formulas

5   Sorting, checking and importing data

This chapter explains some of the built-in tools found in normal spreadsheet packages:
- Formula validation
- Spell check
- Find and replace
- Sorting and filtering data
- Introducing subtotals
- Embedding and linking
- Import/Export

6   Statistical functions and charts

This chapter explains and illustrates some of the statistical functions which you can use, and the types of chart you can create and provides tips for good presentation. It covers:
- Simple statistical functions
- Analysis tools
- Types of charts
- Chart creation

7   Pivot tables and workbook management

This chapter deals with Pivot Tables and other techniques for manipulating data:
- Managing windows – freeze panes
- Working with multiple worksheets and workbooks
- Using Paste Special
- Creating and formatting pivot tables
- Using subsets of data
- What-if scenarios
- Goal seeking
- Data tables

Practice exercises

Learning about spreadsheet software is an essentially practical process and this book contains a wide range of practical exercises which will enable students to gain the spreadsheet skills needed to tackle the AAT assessment. These exercises and details of their contents are set out on the next page.

Some exercises require the download of spreadsheet files from www.osbornebooks.co.uk ('Resources'). These files are in Excel (2010) format and are also provided as csv files.

List of practice exercises

Notes for tutors

what this book covers

This book has been written specifically to cover the 'Spreadsheet software' Unit which is mandatory for the AAT Level 3 Diploma in Accounting.

The book contains clear and practical explanations of how to create and manipulate spreadsheets.

Each chapter is followed by a set of graded exercises which will enable students to develop and practise their spreadsheet skills.

To speed up the learning process in the later exercises, Osborne Books has provided a number of spreadsheet files for free download from its website www.osbornebooks.co.uk. Access to these can be gained through the 'Resources' button on the menu bar and then via the *Working with Spreadsheets Tutorial* book page.

which spreadsheet software?

The illustrations in this text are based on Excel 2010, part of the Microsoft Office suite, but it is appreciated that a variety of software will be in use at any one time. The text therefore aims to be generic wherever possible so that all users can be catered for.

Note that the downloads referred to above are provided in three versions:

- Excel 2010 and Excel 2007 files – which can be opened in other branded software as appropriate
- CSV files – which can be used to import the required raw data into most spreadsheet programs

AAT sample assessment material

Osborne Books is grateful to the AAT for permission to reproduce sample assessment material at the end of this book. This was current at the time of publication (July 2013) but tutors should check with the AAT website (www.aat.org.uk) to ensure that they have the latest version of this material.

Spreadsheets can be applied to any task that involves numbers and they are commonly used in the areas of accounting, budgeting, planning, financial analysis, and scientific fields. Examples of accounting applications include:

- cashflow planning
- budgeting
- costing
- sales forecasting

- trial balance
- producing the statement of profit or loss and statement of financial position
- simple book-keeping
- sales/purchases and returns daybooks
- bank reconciliation statements
- customer sales analysis
- product sales analysis
- producing quotations

1 Spreadsheet basics

this chapter covers...

This chapter is an introduction for those new to spreadsheets. It explains and takes you through some of the basic concepts and techniques for working with spreadsheets.

By the time you have finished this chapter and carried out the exercises which follow, you should be competent in setting up and manipulating a basic spreadsheet. The concepts and techniques covered are:

■ useful tips

■ basic spreadsheet structure

■ dealing with worksheets

■ dealing with workbooks

■ entering data into cells

■ copying the data in cells

■ dealing with rows and columns

■ changing the height of a row or the width of a column

■ using basic formulas

Note that the the step by step instructions given in this chapter are based on the Microsoft® Excel model, but the concepts and techniques described relate to all spreadsheet packages.

USEFUL TIPS

mouse click

Whenever a CLICK of the mouse is mentioned, this is referring to a click of the LEFT mouse button. Any RIGHT mouse clicks will be specifically preceded by RIGHT. DOUBLE click refers to 2 clicks in quick succession of the LEFT mouse key.

undo

If at any stage you wish to **Undo** the changes which you have just made, click on the **Undo** icon (left pointing curved arrow) to remove the last edit to a cell. To remove the edit before that, click the **Undo** icon again and so on.

help

If you require additional information or clarification on any action, formula or general query, **Help** is available within your spreadsheet program by clicking the **Help** icon (usually a ? symbol).

SPREADSHEET STRUCTURE

definition

A spreadsheet is a grid or table of rows and columns.

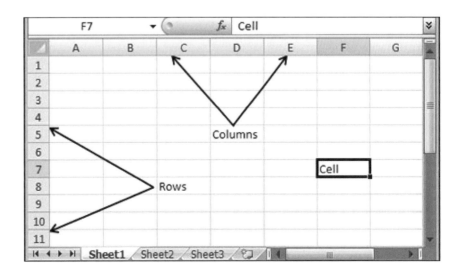

rows, columns and cells

Rows are identified by numbers: 1, 2, 3, and so on.

Columns are identified by letters: A, B, C, and so on.

When columns go beyond Z, they carry on with the letters AA, AB, AC etc.

Where a row and column cross or intersect, it is called a **cell**.

The cell is referred to by a combination of a letter and a number to identify its location known as a **cell reference**.

Cell reference F7 would refer to cell at the intersection of column F (the sixth column) and row 7. See the cell highlighted on the screen image above.

WORKBOOKS AND WORKSHEETS

A **workbook** is the computer file created when you start a new spreadsheet.

A **workbook** contains a set of **worksheets**.

Each **worksheet** is an individual **spreadsheet**.

files and folders

Each workbook is held as one file. A file is the computer equivalent of a paper document containing the information which you have entered. Each file has a name which you specify when it is created. This should be chosen to be meaningful and help identify what the file contains, for example Timesheet March 2013.

To organise our files in a logical way we store related files in a **folder**, which we again name when we create it to clarify the sort of files/documents the folder will contain. For example: Timesheets 2012-2013.

Within Excel the File and Folder tools mentioned below are available whenever you select one of the menu options such as OPEN or SAVE AS which are located under the FILE menu.

create a folder

Creating a folder can be achieved by using the **New Folder** option, and naming the folder appropriately.

finding a file

If you are unable to locate a file, you can use the **Search tool** provided when you select OPEN within the FILE menu.

renaming a file

To rename a file, click the filename, once then once more and type in the new name. Press **RETURN** or click somewhere else to complete the edit. **ESC** will cancel the edit.

sharing a file

To allow the sharing of a file, the file needs to be in a folder which is accessible to other people. By right mouse clicking on the folder name, and setting the **share with** options as required, you can specify who can access the file.

worksheets

Each **worksheet** has a name, which is usually displayed as a tab at the bottom of the spreadsheet work area.

When you create a new workbook it will normally contain 3 worksheets – named Sheet1, Sheet2 and Sheet3.

Worksheet **names** can be changed, usually by double clicking on the name tab, and entering the required text of the new name.

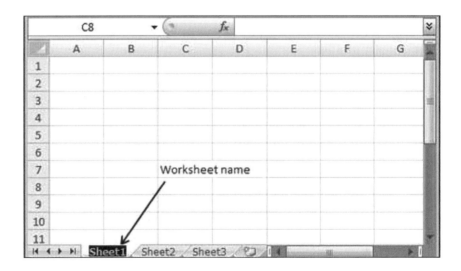

It is possible to add one or more additional worksheets should you require them.

New worksheets are added one at a time, either by clicking on the sheet tab which has no name, but has the standard Windows symbol for a "new" item, or by using **Insert**, and selecting **Worksheet**.

Add new worksheet

Worksheets which are not required can be deleted, by using **Delete** and selecting the worksheet, or right mouse clicking on the sheet to be deleted, and select **Delete**.

You can easily change the relative order of the worksheets within the workbook, just by selecting the name tab, holding the mouse down, and dragging the worksheet to its new position in the order.

Each worksheet can represent one spreadsheet, or data from different worksheets may be linked together to form one more complex spreadsheet.

Switching between worksheets is achieved by clicking on the name tab of the worksheet to which you want to see on the screen.

workbooks

As noted earlier, a **workbook** is a collection of worksheets ranging from one worksheet upwards to a maximum number which will be dependent on the software package and available computer memory.

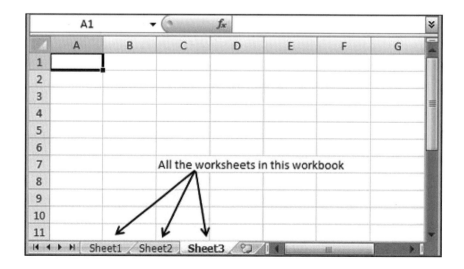

All the worksheets in this workbook

For example, a workbook could have two worksheets, one worksheet with data, and a second worksheet containing a chart representing the data.

When you want to start your first spreadsheet, you will select **New** from the File menu, select **Blank Workbook** from the available templates, and a new workbook will open, usually containing 3 blank worksheets ready for you to enter data.

The information which you have entered should be regularly saved using the standard disk icon, or **Save** under the File menu.

To open a previously saved workbook, you would either select **Open** from the File menu, navigate to the required folder and select the required workbook from the appropriate folder, or if it is listed, select the workbook from the list of recently used documents.

To save a copy of the workbook with a different name either as a backup or as a fresh starting point, you would use **Save as** usually found under the File menu and supply a new name for the copy of the workbook. For security purposes a copy of an important workbook should be saved to removable media such as a memory stick and stored off-site.

It is also good practise to add a version number or part of a date to the filename so that different versions can be saved as the spreadsheet evolves. This also allows a previous version to be identified and opened, if required.

ENTER DATA INTO CELLS

Within the grid of cells on your worksheet, you can move around from cell to cell using various methods:

- the mouse

- the arrow keys

- the **TAB** key

- or the **RETURN** key (also known as the **ENTER** key)

The current cell, known as the active cell is highlighted.

The active cell reference is shown in the **Name Box** above column A; this is E5 in the example on the next page.

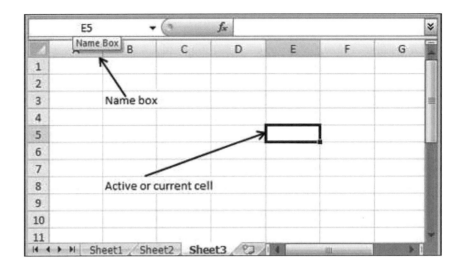

To enter data into a cell:

■ click on the cell where you want the data to go

■ type your data into the cell

■ either press the **RETURN** key, or click on another cell with the mouse

Other useful keys when entering data are the **TAB** key which moves the active cell to the next cell in the current row, and the **ESC** key which cancels the current data entry.

If you just wish to edit the current data, you will see the data held in the current cell displayed in the **Formula Bar**, (in this example Expenditure forecast).

To modify the contents of a cell:

- click on the required cell
- either enter the new data directly
- *or* click into the Formula Bar
- make any changes
- press **RETURN**

If at any time you wish to cancel the changes, press the **ESC** key before pressing **RETURN**.

To remove data:

- select the cell to be changed
- press the **Delete** key
- *or* select **Clear Contents** from the drop down menu displayed when you right mouse click on the cell

selecting multiple cells

If at any time you wish to select more than one cell:

- select the first cell by clicking on the cell
- keep the left mouse button pressed and drag the mouse over the other cells you wish to select

A series of selected cells is shown below.

January	March	April	May	June	

If the cells you wish to select are not consecutive (i.e. next to each other)

- select the first cell by clicking on the cell
- hold down the **CONTROL** key while clicking on the other cells you want to select

It is often useful to be able to select multiple cells as you will see in the following sections.

COPYING CELLS

The simplest method of copying data in a cell is to:

- move to the cell you wish to copy
- from the Home menu, select **Copy**
- move to the cell where you wish to place the copy
- from the Home menu select **Paste**.

If you wish to paste the data into more than one cell, select all the cells where the data is to go, then select **Paste**.

Alternatively, to copy the selected cell, you could click on the **Copy** icon on the tool bar if there is one, or press **CTRL** and **C** together; then to paste, click on the **Paste** icon, or press **CTRL** and **V** together.

It is also possible to move the contents of one cell to a new cell reference:

- click on the data cell to move
- hold the left mouse button down, you will see an outline moving with the mouse
- move to the cell where the data is to go
- release the mouse

You will see the data move to the new location.

If at any time you wish to copy more than one cell at a time:

- select the cells to copy by clicking on the first cell
- keeping the left mouse key pressed drag the mouse in the appropriate direction until all the required cells are selected
- select **Copy** and **Paste** as described above

Alternatively, click on the first cell, move to the last of the cells to be selected, hold down the **SHIFT** key and click the mouse.

If the cells which you wish to copy are not consecutive, for each of the cells to be copied, hold down the **CTRL** key and click the cell, as described in the section on selecting multiple cells.

DEALING WITH ROWS AND COLUMNS

On a worksheet, each column is identified by a letter or combination of letters; this is called the **Column header**.

Similarly each row is identified by a number called the **Row header**.

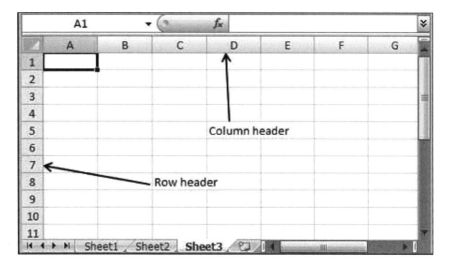

One click on a column header will select the entire column. Similarly with a row header, one click on the row header will select the whole row.

If you realise that you have missed out a row or a column once you have entered data, it is straightforward to insert extra rows or columns.

inserting a column

■ select the column to the right of where you want to insert another column, by right clicking on the column header

■ select **Insert** from the menu displayed

The new column will be inserted at the position of the selected column, and all existing columns will move right, as shown in the example below. You can then enter data in the new column.

Note that for some spreadsheet packages you may need to select **Insert**, then **Column** from the menus.

	A	B	C	D	E	F	G
1	Expenditure forecast						
2							
3		January	February	March	April	May	June
4							
5	Salaries						
6	Rent						
7	Accountancy						
8	Advertising						

inserting a row

■ select the row below where you want to insert another row, by right clicking on the row header

■ select **Insert** from the menu displayed; for some spreadsheet packages you may need to select **Insert**, then **Row** from the menu

In the two screens below a new row 'Insurance' has been inserted between the rows for Salaries and Rent (rows 5 and 6). Note that the new row will be inserted at the selected row (row 6), and all the existing rows will then move down. You can then enter data in the new row.

3		January	February	March	April	May	June
4							
5	Salaries						
6	Rent						
7	Accountancy						

3		January	February	March	April	May	June
4							
5	Salaries						
6	Insurance						
7	Rent						
8	Accountancy						

For some spreadsheet packages you may need to select **Insert**, then **Row** from the menus.

deleting a column

To delete a column:

■ select the column to be deleted, by right clicking on the column header

■ select **Delete** from the menu displayed.

For some spreadsheet packages you may need to select **Delete**, then **Column** from the menus.

deleting a row

To delete a row:

- select the row to be deleted, by right clicking on the row header

- select **Delete** from the menu displayed

For some spreadsheet packages you may need to select **Delete**, then **Row** from the menus.

changing the width of a column

A8	▼		fx	Accountancy			≫
	A	B	C	D	E	F	G
1	Expenditure forecast						
2							
3		January	February	March	April	May	June
4							
5	Salaries						
6	Insurance						
7	Rent						
8	Accountancy						
9	Advertising						
10	Postage						
11	Stationery						

Sheet1 Sheet2 **Sheet3**

If you look at the example above, you will see that some of the text in the selected cell in column A overflows into column B. Once we put data into column B, the full text in column A will no longer be visible, so we need to make column A wider.

To make a column wider:

- click on the column header

- move the cursor to the line at the right edge of the column header box, the cursor changes shape to a black cross with arrow heads

- press the mouse down

- drag to the right as far as is required to display all information correctly

- release the mouse

Column A is then made wider, as shown on the next page:

A8		f_x	Accountancy			
	A	B	C	D	E	F	G
1	Expenditure forecast						
2							
3		January	February	March	April	May	June
4							
5	Salaries						
6	Insurance						
7	Rent						
8	Accountancy						
9	Advertising						
10	Postage						
11	Stationery						

Sheet1 Sheet2 **Sheet3**

There are several alternative ways to make a column wider. If you double click on the column header box, the column will automatically widen to contain the longest data within the column.

Also if you right click on the column header, you can select **Column Width** from the drop down menu and specify a width.

changing the height of a row

The method used to modify the height of a row is very similar:

■ click on the row header

■ move the cursor to the bottom edge of the row header box, the cursor changes shape to a black cross with arrow heads

■ press the mouse down

■ drag down or up until you are satisfied with the row height

■ release the mouse

USING BASIC FORMULAS

The most powerful feature of a spreadsheet is its ability to perform calculations. To **create a formula**, click on the cell where you wish to place the formula. Enter the "=" sign to indicate that this cell is going to contain a formula. The formula can contain numbers, cell references and arithmetic symbols, eg '+' as shown below:

A simple formula for **addition** might be something like

$$=B4+B5+B6+42$$

This would add up the values in the cells B4, B5, B6 and the number 42.

A simple formula for **subtraction** is: =B4–B5

For **multiplication**: =B4*B5

And **division**: =B4/B5

To make one cell always hold the same value as another, eg B2 having the same value as A1, enter the formula =A1 in cell B2.

In the example below, we want to enter formulas to calculate the totals for each month.

	A	B	C	D	E	F	G	H
	B11	▼		f_x =				
1	Expenditure forecast							
2								
3		January	February	March	April	May	June	
4	Salaries	£80,000	£80,000	£80,000	£90,000	£90,000	£90,000	
5	Insurance	£1,000	£500	£0	£0	£0	£500	
6	Rent	£3,500	£3,500	£3,500	£3,500	£3,500	£3,500	
7	Accountancy	£270	£0	£270	£0	£270	£0	
8	Advertising	£0	£1,500	£0	£0	£0	£1,800	
9	Postage	£95	£190	£95	£80	£95	£150	
10	Stationery	£57	£90	£0	£90	£0	£90	
11	Totals	=						

H ◀ ▶ H Sheet1 Sheet2 Sheet3

The formula we could enter in cell B11 to add up column B, would be
$$=B4+B5+B6+B7+B8+B9+B10$$

There is an alternative way of adding these numbers, using the built-in function **SUM( )**

The equivalent formula would be =SUM(B4:B10) which will add up all the cells from B4 to B10 inclusive.

This formula could then be copied to each of the cells in the Totals row in each column to produce a monthly total for the expenditure forecast, using **Copy** and **Paste** as described previously.

Note that as the formula is copied to the new cells it will **automatically change** to reflect the new row/column references.

B11				fx	=SUM(B4:B10)			
	A	B	C	D	E	F	G	H
1	Expenditure forecast							
2								
3		January	February	March	April	May	June	Average
4	Salaries	£80,000	£80,000	£80,000	£90,000	£90,000	£90,000	
5	Insurance	£1,000	£500	£0	£0	£0	£500	
6	Rent	£3,500	£3,500	£3,500	£3,500	£3,500	£3,500	
7	Accountancy	£270	£0	£270	£0	£270	£0	
8	Advertising	£0	£1,500	£0	£0	£0	£1,800	
9	Postage	£95	£190	£95	£80	£95	£150	
10	Stationery	£57	£90	£0	£90	£0	£90	
11	Totals	£84,922	£85,780	£83,865	£93,670	£93,865	£96,040	

H ◀ ▶ H   Sheet1 Sheet2 Sheet3

calculating averages

As you can see from Column H in the screen above, the next requirement is to calculate the **average expenditure** for each expense type over the six months. To do this we could can use the function **AVERAGE**.

The formula in this case would be =AVERAGE(B4:G4). This calculates the average value of all cells from B4 to G4 inclusively.

Again, this formula can be copied to all the other cells in the Average column, producing the results shown below in Column H.

H4				fx	=AVERAGE(B4:G4)			
	A	B	C	D	E	F	G	H
1	Expenditure forecast							
2								
3		January	February	March	April	May	June	Average
4	Salaries	£80,000	£80,000	£80,000	£90,000	£90,000	£90,000	£85,000
5	Insurance	£1,000	£500	£0	£0	£0	£500	£333
6	Rent	£3,500	£3,500	£3,500	£3,500	£3,500	£3,500	£3,500
7	Accountancy	£270	£0	£270	£0	£270	£0	£135
8	Advertising	£0	£1,500	£0	£0	£0	£1,800	£550
9	Postage	£95	£190	£95	£80	£95	£150	£118
10	Stationery	£57	£90	£0	£90	£0	£90	£55
11	Totals	£84,922	£85,780	£83,865	£93,670	£93,865	£96,040	

H ◀ ▶ H   Sheet1 Sheet2 Sheet3

There are many built-in functions which are available to use within your spreadsheet. A number of these will be covered in subsequent chapters.

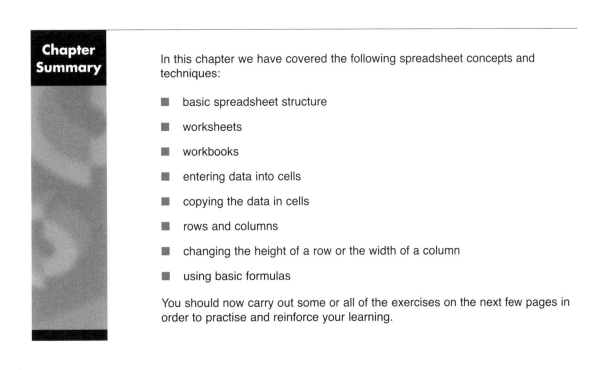

Chapter Summary

In this chapter we have covered the following spreadsheet concepts and techniques:

- basic spreadsheet structure

- worksheets

- workbooks

- entering data into cells

- copying the data in cells

- rows and columns

- changing the height of a row or the width of a column

- using basic formulas

You should now carry out some or all of the exercises on the next few pages in order to practise and reinforce your learning.

Activities

Exercise 1 – setting up a new worksheet

In this first exercise we will create a simple spreadsheet to record time worked on various activities.

Stage 1

This stage is all about entering some text to form the basic layout of our spreadsheet

1. Open a new workbook.
2. Move to Sheet1.
3. Change the name of the sheet to **Time data**.
4. Move to cell A1, enter **Work bookings**.
5. Move to cell A2, enter **Client**.
6. Enter **Week1, Week2, Week3** in cells B2, C2, D2 respectively.
7. Enter **Smiths Ltd, Jones and Partner, Redwoods, Underhills** in cells A3, A4, A5, A6 respectively.
8. Save the workbook with the name **Exercise1**.

Your spreadsheet should appear as shown in the screen below:

	A	B	C	D	E	F	G
1	Work bookings						
2	Client	Week1	Week2	Week3			
3	Smiths Ltd						
4	Jones and Partner						
5	Redwoods						
6	Underhills						
7							
8							
9							

A1   fx   Work bookings

Time data / Sheet2 / Sheet3

Stage 2

We are going to improve the layout and enter some values.

1. Widen column A to allow for the longest entry in column A.

2. Insert a row below Work bookings to improve the presentation.

3. For Smiths Ltd, enter the value **15** for Week1 (cell B4), copy this value into Week2 (cell C4), and Week3 (cell D4).

4. Similarly for Jones and Partner, enter the following values **12, 8, 10**.

5. For Redwoods enter **13, 20, 11**.

6. The values for Underhills are the same as those for Redwoods. Use Copy and Paste to put these values in cells B7, C7, D7.

7. Save your spreadsheet (keeping the same name: **Exercise1**).

Your spreadsheet should appear as shown in the screen below:

	A1		f_x	Work bookings		
	A	B	C	D	E	F
1	Work bookings					
2						
3	Client	Week1	Week2	Week3		
4	Smiths Ltd	15	15	15		
5	Jones and Partner	12	8	10		
6	Redwoods	13	20	11		
7	Underhills	13	20	11		
8						
9						

Time data / Sheet2 / Sheet3

Stage 3

We are now going to use some formulas to get the spreadsheet to do some calculations for us.

1. In cell A9 enter **Totals**.

2. Cell B9 is the first cell where we want to enter the formula to total cells B4 through to B7 (using the SUM function).

3. Copy the formula from cell B9 into C9 and D9 to calculate the other totals.

4. Save your spreadsheet.

Your spreadsheet should appear as shown in the screen at the top of the next page.

	B9	▼		f_x	=SUM(B4:B7)		
	A	B	C	D	E	F	
1	Work bookings						
2							
3	Client	Week1	Week2	Week3			
4	Smiths Ltd	15	15	15			
5	Jones and Partner	12	8	10			
6	Redwoods	13	20	11			
7	Underhills	13	20	11			
8							
9	Totals	53	63	47			

Time data / Sheet2 / Sheet3

Stage 4

One more calculation is needed.

1. In cell E3 enter **Average**.

2. Cell E4 is the first cell where we want to enter the formula to calculate the average of cells B4 through to D4.

3. Copy the formula from cell E4 into E5 through to E7 to calculate the other averages.

4. Save your spreadsheet.

The final spreadsheet is shown below.

	E4	▼		f_x	=AVERAGE(B4:D4)		
	A	B	C	D	E	F	
1	Work bookings						
2							
3	Client	Week1	Week2	Week3	Average		
4	Smiths Ltd	15	15	15	15		
5	Jones and Partner	12	8	10	10		
6	Redwoods	13	20	11	14.66667		
7	Underhills	13	20	11	14.66667		
8							
9	Totals	53	63	47			

Time data / Sheet2 / Sheet3

Exercise 2 – correcting and extending data, adding formulas

In this next exercise we will modify the previous time recording spreadsheet to make some corrections and extend the data recorded.

You will notice that changes to the data automatically change the values in those cells where we have a formula.

Stage 1

This stage involves making changes within an existing spreadsheet.

1. Open the workbook created in the previous exercise **Exercise1**.

2. Save the workbook with a new name **Exercise2**.

3. Week2 for Smiths Ltd should read **5** not 15, change the value in cell C4.

4. Week2 for Underhills should read **12** not 20, change the value in cell C7.

5. Underhills should be **Underhills Ltd**, change the entry in cell A7.

6. Change all the text in row 3 to capital letters (these are our headings within the spreadsheet).

7. Save the workbook still with the name **Exercise2**.

Your spreadsheet should appear as shown in the screen below.

	A	B	C	D	E	F	G
	A1		f_x	Work bookings			
1	Work bookings						
2							
3	CLIENT	WEEK1	WEEK2	WEEK3	AVERAGE		
4	Smiths Ltd	15	5	15	11.66667		
5	Jones and Partner	12	8	10	10		
6	Redwoods	13	20	11	14.66667		
7	Underhills Ltd	13	12	11	12		
8							
9	Totals	53	45	47			
10							
11							

Time data / Sheet2 / Sheet3

Stage 2

We are going to enter some additional values because we now have data for Week4, and a new client.

1. Insert a column after Week3 and before Average (between columns D and E).

2. Enter text **WEEK4** in cell E3.

3. Time booking for each client for Week4 is **6** hours. Use Copy and Paste to enter **6** in cells E4, E5, E6 and E7.

4. Enter the formula for the total for Week4 in cell E9 (Note: You can either use Copy and Paste to copy the formula from one of the other Total cells, or enter the formula using Sum, and include all cells from E4 through to E7.

5. A new client was taken on in Week4. Insert a row below Underhills Ltd, still leaving a blank row above Totals.

6. The new client name is Abbey Builders. Enter **Abbey Builders** in cell A8.

7. For Abbey Builders, enter the value **0** for Week1 (cell B8), copy this value into Week2 (cell C8), and Week3 (cell D8) and then enter the value **13** into Week4 (cell E8).

8. Check the formulas for Totals for each week, making sure they include the new row (Abbey Builders in Row 8). Modify and copy across to each week if necessary.

9. Save your spreadsheet.

Your spreadsheet should now look as shown below:

	B10			f_x	=SUM(B4:B8)			
	A	B	C	D	E	F	G	
1	Work bookings							
2								
3	CLIENT	WEEK1	WEEK2	WEEK3	WEEK4	AVERAGE		
4	Smiths Ltd	15	5	15	6	10.25		
5	Jones and Partner	12	8	10	6	9		
6	Redwoods	13	20	11	6	12.5		
7	Underhills Ltd	13	12	11	6	10.5		
8	Abbey Builders	0	0	0	13			
9								
10	Totals	53	45	47	37			
11								

Time data Sheet2 Sheet3

Stage 3

We are now going to introduce some more formulas to get the spreadsheet to do some additional calculations for us.

1. We no longer need the Average column. Delete column F.

2. We want to calculate the total number of hours for each client. Enter **CLIENT TOTAL** in cell F3.

3. Widen column F so that the **CLIENT TOTAL** text fits within the column.

4. Enter the formula in cell F4 to total cells B4 through to E4.

5. Copy the formula from cell F4 into cells F5, F6, F7, and F8 to calculate the other totals.

6. Enter **EXTENDED** in cell G3.

7. Widen column G so that the text fits within the column.

8. Each client total is to be multiplied by 1.5. Enter the formula in G4 to give Smiths Ltd total (F4) multiplied by 1.5.

9. Copy the formula from F4 into cells F5,F6,F7,F8.

10. Save your spreadsheet.

Your spreadsheet should look as shown below:

G4	▼	f_x	=F4*1.5				⊗
Name Box	B	C	D	E	F	G	
1 Work bookings							
2							
3 CLIENT	WEEK1	WEEK2	WEEK3	WEEK4	CLIENT TOTAL	EXTENDED	
4 Smiths Ltd	15	5	15	6	41	61.5	
5 Jones and Partner	12	8	10	6	36	54	
6 Redwoods	13	20	11	6	50	75	
7 Underhills Ltd	13	12	11	6	42	63	
8 Abbey Builders	0	0	0	13	13	19.5	
9							
10 Totals	53	45	47	37			
11							
⊮ ◀ ▶ ⊳ Time data	Sheet2	Sheet3	⌘				

Exercise 3 – creating another workbook, using formulas to check data

In this exercise we will create simple spreadsheet for bank transactions.

Stage 1

This stage involves entering some text to form the basic layout of our spreadsheet.

1. Open a new workbook.

2. Move to Sheet2.

3. Change the name of the sheet to **July**.

4. Move to cell A1, enter **Bank transactions**.

5. Move to cell A3, enter **Opening balance**.

6. Widen column A so that all text is contained within the column.

7. Enter **1500** in cell B3.

8. Enter **Date** in cell A5, **Debit** in B5, **Credit** in C5, **Balance** in D5.

9. Save the workbook with the name **Exercise3**.

Your spreadsheet should look as shown below:

	A	B	C	D	E	F	G	H
	A5		f_x Date					
1	Bank transactions							
2								
3	Opening balance	1500						
4								
5	Date	Debit	Credit	Balance				
6								
7								
8								
9								
10								
11								

Sheet1 **July** Sheet3

Stage 2

We are going to enter details of some transactions.

1. Starting in row 6 enter **02/07/10** in column A, **95.34** in column B, **0** in column C.

2. In row 7, enter **11/07/10**, **0**, **25.5** in columns A, B, C respectively.

3. In row 8, enter **15/07/10**, **0**, **34.78** in columns A, B, C respectively.

4. In row 9, enter **22/07/10**, **67.99**, **0** in columns A, B, C respectively.

5. In row 10, enter **28/07/10**, **17.99**, **0** in columns A, B, C respectively.

6. Save your spreadsheet.

Your spreadsheet should now look as shown below:

	C10			f_x 0					
	A	B	C	D	E	F	G	H	
1	Bank transactions								
2									
3	Opening balance	1500							
4									
5	Date	Debit	Credit	Balance					
6	02/07/2010	95.34	0						
7	11/07/2010	0	25.5						
8	15/07/2010	0	34.78						
9	22/07/2010	67.99	0						
10	28/07/2010	17.99	0						
11									
	Sheet1 July Sheet3								

Stage 3

We are now going to enter some formulas to calculate the balance after each transaction.

1. On the first row of data (row 6) the value in the Balance column is going to be calculated using the opening balance. Enter a formula in cell D6, which takes the opening balance (B3), subtracts the debit (B6), and adds the credit (C6).

2. Enter the formula in D7, which uses the previous balance from D6, subtracts the debit (B7), and adds the credit (C7).

3. Enter a formula for the remaining rows of data.

4. Save your spreadsheet.

Your spreadsheet should now look as shown below:

	D6			f_x	=B3-B6+C6				
	A	B	C	D	E	F	G	H	
1	Bank transactions								
2									
3	Opening balance	1500							
4									
5	Date	Debit	Credit	Balance					
6	02/07/2010	95.34	0	1404.66					
7	11/07/2010	0	25.5	1430.16					
8	15/07/2010	0	34.78	1464.94					
9	22/07/2010	67.99	0	1396.95					
10	28/07/2010	17.99	0	1378.96					
11									
12									

Sheet1   **July**   Sheet3

Stage 4

We are now going to finalise the spreadsheet and enter some formulas to carry out some cross checks.

1. Enter **Closing balance** in cell A4.

2. Insert a row between row 4 and row 5.

3. The value of the closing balance will be the balance after the last transaction (D11 in this instance). Enter a formula in B4 so that this cell always holds the value of D11.

4. The transaction of 28/07/10 is incorrect, the Debit figure should be 107.99. Change the value in cell B11; see how the value in B4 changes to the new closing balance figure.

5. Enter **Totals** in cell A12.

6. Enter a formula in cell B12 to total the debits. (Adding up B7 through to B11).

7. Enter a formula in cell C12 to total the credits.

8. In cell E12, enter a formula which takes the opening balance, subtracts the total debits, and adds in the total credits. (This should give the same value as the closing balance – a useful reconciliation).

9. Save your spreadsheet.

Your spreadsheet should now appear as shown below:

	E12			f_x	=B3-B12+C12				
	A	B	C	D	E	F	G	H	
1	Bank transactions								
2									
3	Opening balance	1500							
4	Closing balance	1288.96							
5									
6	Date	Debit	Credit	Balance					
7	02/07/2010	95.34	0	1404.66					
8	11/07/2010	0	25.5	1430.16					
9	15/07/2010	0	34.78	1464.94					
10	22/07/2010	67.99	0	1396.95					
11	28/07/2010	107.99	0	1288.96					
12	Totals	271.32	60.28		1288.96				
13									

Sheet1   **July**   Sheet3

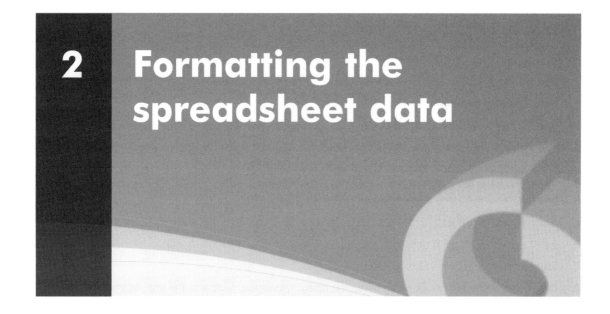

2 **Formatting the spreadsheet data**

this chapter covers...

In this chapter we describe ways of formatting data within a spreadsheet using different text fonts and styles. We also explain different ways of representing numeric data, including currencies and dates. Page layouts will also be explained.

When you have finished this chapter and carried out the exercises which follow, you should be competent in formatting and also printing a spreadsheet.

The concepts and techniques covered are:

■ *formatting – style*

■ *formatting – fonts and size*

■ *number formats*

■ *cell alignments*

■ *date formats*

■ *printing and page setup*

Note that the the step-by-step instructions given in this chapter are based on the Microsoft® Excel model, but the concepts and techniques described relate to all spreadsheet packages.

FORMATTING – STYLE

Text formatting within a spreadsheet, as with other types of document, is often used to make an item stand out or to emphasise specific data.

We will use the expenditure worksheet shown below as an example.

A1			f_x	Expenditure forecast				
	A	B	C	D	E	F	G	H
1	Expenditure forecast							
2								
3		January	February	March	April	May	June	
4								
5	Salaries							
6	Insurance							
7	Rent							
8	Accountancy							
9	Advertising							
10	Postage							
11	Stationery							
12								
13								

Sheet1 / Sheet2 / Sheet3

making data bold

To make data bold:

■ click on the required cell

then

■ click on the **Bold** icon on the menu bar if visible

or

■ right click on the selected cell

■ select **Format cells**

■ select **Font**

■ make the font style **Bold**

or

■ press **CTRL** and **B** together (hold down the **CONTROL** key and tap the **B** key and release)

Now look at the next page to see the result.

	A	B	C	D	E	F	G	H
1	Expenditure forecast							
2								
3		January	February	March	April	May	June	
4								
5	Salaries							
6	Insurance							
7	Rent							
8	Accountancy		Now bold					
9	Advertising							
10	Postage							
11	Stationery							
12								
13								

Sheet1 Sheet2 **Sheet3**

To make **more than one cell bold**:

- select all the required cells

- and follow the steps set out on on the previous page

using italics

To use **italics in one cell**,

- click on the required cell

then

- click on the *Italics* icon on the menu bar if visible

or

- right click on the selected cell

- select **Format cells**

- select **Font**

- make the font style *Italics*

or

- press **CTRL** and **I** together (hold down the **CONTROL** key and tap the **I** key and release)

See the spreadsheet screen on the top of the next page.

To make **more than one cell italicised:**

- select all the required cells

- and follow one of the formatting choices explained above

underlining data

To **underline data**,

■ click on the required cell

then

■ click on the **Underline** icon on the menu bar if visible

or

■ right click on the selected cell, select **Format cells**, select **Font** and make the underline style **Single**

or

■ press **CTRL** and **U** together (hold down the **CONTROL** key and tap the **U** key and release)

To underline data in more than one cell, select all the required cells and follow the steps set out above.

To **double underline** data,

■ click on the required cell

Then

■ click on the drop down arrow by the <u>U</u>nderline icon

■ select <u>D</u>ouble underline

Or

■ Right click on the selected cell, select **Format cells**, select **Font** and make the underline style **double**

note – changing back to normal text

To turn off the style, such as bold, underline, italics, you follow exactly the same steps described above and the style will change back to normal.

FORMATTING TEXT – FONT AND SIZE

font face

The **font face** (often known as the '**font**') of text is the style of the lettering:

This is Times   This is Helvetica

To change the font face:

■ click on the required cell

then

■ click on the **Font face list** dropdown on the menu bar if visible

■ select the required font face

or

■ right click on the selected cell

■ select **Format cells**

■ select **Font**

■ choose the required **Font face** from the list

To change the font face in more than one cell, select all the required cells and follow the steps above.

font size

To change the font size

■ click on the required cell

then

■ click on the **Font size** dropdown on the menu bar if visible

■ select the required font face size

or

■ right click on the selected cell, select **Format cells**, select **Font** and choose the required font size from the list

To change the font size in more than one cell, select all the required cells and follow the steps above.

FORMATTING – NUMBERS

The word '**format**' is used in this context to describe the way in which a number will be displayed.

dealing with decimal places

When you enter a number into a cell it is displayed exactly as you type it, except that any **trailing zeros** (zeros after the last non-zero digit on the right of the decimal point), and **leading zeros** (zeros before the first non-zero digit at the front of the number) will be ignored.

For example, if you type **0000125.76000** into a cell and press **RETURN** (Enter) you will see **125.76** displayed.

If you want to see trailing zeros after a decimal point, you will need to change the number of decimal places which are displayed.

For example, if you are dealing with money amounts, you will want to see £34.10 rather than £34.1, which looks very odd. Therefore it is quite common that you would want all values in a particular column or row to display to a certain number of decimal places, to give a consistent view to the spreadsheet.

You can see in the example below that several of the data entries are displayed with only one digit after the decimal point.

6	Date	Debit	Credit	Balance			
7	02/07/2010	95.34	0	1404.66			
8	11/07/2010	0	25.5	1430.16			
9	15/07/2010	0	34.78	1464.94			
10	22/07/2010	67.9	0	1397.04			
11	28/07/2010	107.99	0	1289.05			
12	Totals	271.23	60.28		1289.05		
13							

Sheet1 **July** Sheet3

To change the number of decimal places:

- select the required cells, row or column
- right click on the selection
- select **Format cells**
- select the **Number** tab
- select category **Number**
- adjust the number of decimal places as required

You can see the effect below where the number formats for columns B and C have been changed to display 2 decimal places.

	A	B	C	D	E	F	G	H
1	Bank transactions							
2								
3	Opening balance	1500.00						
4	Closing balance	1289.05						
5								
6	Date	Debit	Credit	Balance				
7	02/07/2010	95.34	0.00	1404.66				
8	11/07/2010	0.00	25.50	1430.16				
9	15/07/2010	0.00	34.78	1464.94				
10	22/07/2010	67.90	0.00	1397.04				
11	28/07/2010	107.99	0.00	1289.05				
12	Totals	271.23	60.28		1289.05			
13								

displaying commas in figures

In order to make numbers more readable, we often insert a comma to identify when the number is over a thousand, and a further comma for over a million and so on.

To display a , (comma) to represent thousands:

- select the required cells, row or column
- right click on the selection
- select **Format** cells
- select the **Number** tab
- select **category Number**
- tick the **Use 1000** separator box

As you can see in the image below the comma can make a big difference to the readability of the spreadsheet. Compare Column D below with Column D on the the screen shown on the previous page.

	A	B	C	D	E	F	G	H
1	Bank transactions							
2								
3	Opening balance	1,500.00						
4	Closing balance	1,289.05						
5								
6	Date	Debit	Credit	Balance				
7	02/07/2010	95.34	0.00	1,404.66				
8	11/07/2010	0.00	25.50	1,430.16				
9	15/07/2010	0.00	34.78	1,464.94				
10	22/07/2010	67.90	0.00	1,397.04				
11	28/07/2010	107.99	0.00	1,289.05				
12	Totals	271.23	60.28		1,289.05			
13								

dealing with currencies

Often when we are dealing with money it is simpler to use the built in **Format of currency** for our data. A format of currency does not affect the values but merely the way the data is displayed.

One of the most commonly used currencies is the UK pound sterling.

To display data as **Currency sterling** with a £ symbol

- select the required cells, row or column

- right click on the selection

- select **Format** cells

- select the **Number** tab

- select category **Currency**

- adjust the decimal places as required

- for **Symbol** select the £ (pound sterling) from the list displayed

The effect of formatting columns B, C and D as currency sterling is shown below.

	A	B	C	D	E	F	G	H
	A13			f_x				
1	Bank transactions							
2								
3	Opening balance	£1,500.00						
4	Closing balance	£1,289.05						
5								
6	Date	Debit	Credit	Balance				
7	02/07/2010	£95.34	£0.00	£1,404.66				
8	11/07/2010	£0.00	£25.50	£1,430.16				
9	15/07/2010	£0.00	£34.78	£1,464.94				
10	22/07/2010	£67.90	£0.00	£1,397.04				
11	28/07/2010	£107.99	£0.00	£1,289.05				
12	Totals	£271.23	£60.28		£1,289.05			
13								

Sheet1 July Sheet3

If the values we had entered were euros, we could use the same procedure as for the pound sterling (see above) and select the euro as the symbol from the list displayed. The spreadsheet would then appear as follows:

A13			f_x					
	A	B	C	D	E	F	G	H
1	Bank transactions							
2								
3	Opening balance	€ 1,500.00						
4	Closing balance	€ 1,289.05						
5								
6	Date	Debit	Credit	Balance				
7	02/07/2010	€ 95.34	€ 0.00	€ 1,404.66				
8	11/07/2010	€ 0.00	€ 25.50	€ 1,430.16				
9	15/07/2010	€ 0.00	€ 34.78	€ 1,464.94				
10	22/07/2010	€ 67.90	€ 0.00	€ 1,397.04				
11	28/07/2010	€ 107.99	€ 0.00	€ 1,289.05				
12	Totals	€ 271.23	€ 60.28		€ 1,289.05			
13								

Sheet1 **July** Sheet3

dealing with percentages

It is also possible to display a number as a **percentage** (%).

If you enter numbers followed by a % sign, the data will be recognised as a percentage and the % sign will be displayed.

If you have a calculation, and you want the result to **display as a percentage**, rather than decimals, you would use the format options to change the way the result is displayed. For example you may want to show the closing balance in the spreadsheet on the opposite page as a percentage of the opening balance.

To do this, you would first insert an appropriate text description in cell D4 and then the formula =B4/B3 in cell E4 (see pages 13-14 for formulas) to calculate the closing balance divided by the opening balance.

The spreadsheet would then look like this (note top bar and cells D4 and E4):

E4			f_x =B4/B3				
	A	B	C	D	E	F	G
1	Bank transactions						
2							
3	Opening balance	€ 1,500.00					
4	Closing balance	€ 1,289.05		C.Bal/O.Bal	0.86		
5							
6	Date	Debit	Credit	Balance			
7	02/07/2010	€ 95.34	€ 0.00	€ 1,404.66			
8	11/07/2010	€ 0.00	€ 25.50	€ 1,430.16			
9	15/07/2010	€ 0.00	€ 34.78	€ 1,464.94			
10	22/07/2010	€ 67.90	€ 0.00	€ 1,397.04			
11	28/07/2010	€ 107.99	€ 0.00	€ 1,289.05			
12	Totals	€ 271.23	€ 60.28		€ 1,289.05		
13							

Sheet1 **July** Sheet3

To make cell E4 display as a **percentage**:

- select the required cell

- right click on the selection

- select **Format** cells

- select the **Number** tab

- select category **Percentage**

- adjust the decimal places as required

The spreadsheet will then appear as shown below.

	E4	▼		f_x =B4/B3				
	A	B	C	D	E	F	G	
1	Bank transactions							
2								
3	Opening balance	€1,500.00						
4	Closing balance	€1,289.05		C.Bal/O.Bal	85.94%			
5								
6	Date	Debit	Credit	Balance				
7	02/07/2010	€95.34	€0.00	€1,404.66				
8	11/07/2010	€0.00	€25.50	€1,430.16				
9	15/07/2010	€0.00	€34.78	€1,464.94				
10	22/07/2010	€67.90	€0.00	€1,397.04				
11	28/07/2010	€107.99	€0.00	€1,289.05				
12	Totals	€271.23	€60.28		€1,289.05			
13								

Sheet1 **July** Sheet3

Note: applying a format of percentage will automatically multiply the selected cell (or cells) by 100 to create a percentage.

CELL ALIGNMENT

Alignment is used to describe the relative position of data within a cell.

With **left alignment** the data is shown up against the left edge of the cell.

Right alignment means that the data is shown up against the right edge of the cell.

For **centre alignment** the data is positioned in the centre of the cell.

Examples of all of these are shown in the screen at the top of the next page.

By default any text entered is aligned to the left.

Data which is recognised as a number will be automatically aligned to the right.

To change the way data is aligned in a cell or cells:

- select the required cells, row or column
- right click on the selection
- select **Format** cells
- select the **Alignment** tab
- on the Horizontal dropdown select **Left**, **Right** or **Centre** as required

or with the cells selected

- click on the appropriate **Alignment** icon on the menu bar if visible

merged cells

Sometimes we have some text which we specifically want to spread across several cells, perhaps as a heading, and we may wish it to be centred across these cells.

To achieve this we effectively **merge** the cells together to make one big cell and then apply standard alignment options within this **merged cell**.

You can see in the example above that the merged cells (B6, C6, D6) are now treated as just one cell, when selected, and this allows us to centre the text over the three columns B, C and D.

To merge cells:

■ select the required cells

■ right click on the selection

■ select **Format** cells

■ select the **Alignment** tab

■ on the text control section click the **Merge** cells checkbox

or with the cells selected

■ click on the **Merge** cells icon on the menu bar if visible

DATE FORMATS

There are a variety of different ways in which dates can be displayed.

The common way of describing dates is to use 'd' for day, 'm' for month and 'y' for year.

If we take the date of 10th February 2010, it can be displayed in the following formats (for UK dates):

■ dd/mm/yyyy would display as 10/02/2010

■ dd/mm/yy would display as 10/02/10

To change the way a date is displayed:

■ select the required cells

■ right click on the selection

■ select **Format** cells

■ select the **Number** tab

■ select category **Date**

■ choose the format you require from the dropdown list

The spreadsheet at the top of the next page shows the year date amended from 2010 to 10.

You can also use other date formats which are available under category **Custom**.

A8		f_x	02/07/2010				
	A	B	C	D	E	F	G	H
1	Bank transactions							
2								
3	Opening balance	1500						
4	Closing balance	1289.05						
5								
6			Transactions					
7	Date	Debit	Credit	Balance				
8	02/07/10	95.34	0	1404.66				
9	11/07/10	0	25.5	1430.16				
10	15/07/10	0	34.78	1464.94			Revised date format	
11	22/07/10	67.9	0	1397.04				
12	28/07/10	107.99	0	1289.05				
13	Totals	271.23	60.28		1289.05			

Sheet1   **July**   Sheet3

PAGE SETUP AND PRINTING

Once we have created and formatted our spreadsheet it is quite possible that we will want to print it.

Spreadsheets are not like word-processed documents – they do not automatically fit within one horizontal page width and flow on downwards.

The first step is to see what the spreadsheet would look like when printed, without actually printing. From the **File** menu, select **Print**. You will then see all the print settings which you can change, together with a **Print Preview** of the worksheet on the right hand side of the screen. Alternatively, you can select **Page Setup** from the **Page Layout** menu, then **Print Preview**.

If you need to make adjustments to the layout for printing, this can be done through **Settings** within the **Print** option, or **Page Setup** within the **Page Layout** menu.

Page Setup allows you to:

■ change the **orientation**, so if the spreadsheet is slightly too wide to fit on one page width, you might change the orientation to **Landscape**

■ adjust the **Margins** – you might want to reduce these to a minimum to give as much space as possible

■ select **Fit to page** – you can specify how many pages wide, by how many pages tall you want to fit the spreadsheet into; it is important to make sure that the text of the spreadsheet remains legible

■ check or uncheck the **gridlines** box if you want to see gridlines for the rows and columns included on your printout.

The two images below show print previews where the page orientations are:

- portrait – one is taller than it is wider – like a portrait picture
- landscape – the other is wider than it is taller – like a landscape painting

The image below shows a print preview where the page orientation is **Portrait**.

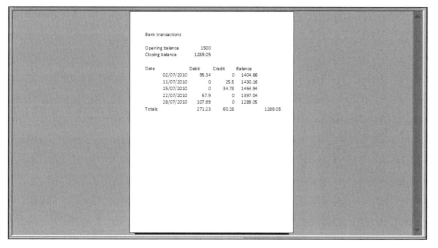

The image below shows a print preview where the page orientation is **Landscape**.

headers and footers

It is sometimes useful to add a **header** or a **footer** to your spreadsheet.

As you would expect a **header** is something which will usually appear at the top of each page when printed, this could be something like "Company Confidential" and the date.

A **footer** will appear at the bottom and is often used to include the author and a page number if the printing covers more than one page.

To create a header or a footer:

■ select **Page** setup

■ select **Header/Footer**

■ either select one of the built in choices from the drop down list for the header or footer such as page number or date

■ or create your own custom piece of text

An example of the Page setup found within Microsoft® Excel is shown below

If we wish to format our printed output so that part of the information is on one page and the remainder on another page, we can insert what is known as a page break.

To insert a page break:

■ select the **Page Layout** menu

■ click on the cell to be the start of the new page

■ select **Breaks**

■ select **Insert Page Break**.

Other packages will usually provide the same facilities presented in a different way. We recommend that you experiment and gain an understanding of the page setup options.

Chapter Summary

This chapter has covered in detail the following topics:

- formatting –style

- formatting – fonts and size

- number formats

- cell alignments

- date formats

- page setup

You should now carry out some or all of the exercises on the next few pages in order to practise and reinforce your learning.

Activities

Exercise 1 – using percentages and averages

In this first exercise we will create a simple spreadsheet to record exam results for a group of students.

Stage 1

This stage is about creating the basic layout of our spreadsheet.

All text should be entered in the default typeface, font size 10, normal style.

1.   Open a new workbook

2.   Move to Sheet1

3.   Change the name of the sheet to **Results**

4.   Move to cell A1, enter **Midterm exams**

5.   Move to cell A2, enter **Name**

6.   Enter **Module1, Module2, Module3** in cells B2, C2, D2 respectively

7.   Enter **John Smith, Peter Jones, Wendy Owen, Frank Waters, Barbara White** in cells A3, A4, A5, A6 and A7 respectively

8.   Widen column A to allow for the longest entry in the column

9.   Insert a row between rows 1 and 2 to improve the presentation

10.   Save the workbook with the name **T2Exercise1**

Your spreadsheet should appear as shown in the image below:

Stage 2

We are going to enter some values and format some of the text.

1. For John Smith enter the value **75%** for Module1 (cell B4), **62%** for Module2 (cell C4) and **45%** for Module3 (D4).

2. Similarly for Peter Jones, enter the following values **61%, 48%, 70%**

3. For Wendy Owen, enter **63%, 80%, 51%**

4. For Frank Waters, enter **53%, 85%, 41%**

5. For Barbara White, enter **42%, 63%, 85%**

6. Change the font size of the title in Cell A1 to **16**.

7. Increase the height of row 1 to allow for the larger text.

8. Make all text in row3 (your data headings) bold and underlined.

9. Save your spreadsheet (keeping the same name – **T2Exercise1**).

Your spreadsheet should now appear as shown below:

A9				*fx*				
	A	**B**	**C**	**D**	**E**	**F**	**G**	**H**
1	Midterm exams							
2								
3	Name	Module1	Module2	Module3				
4	John Smith	75%	62%	45%				
5	Peter Jones	61%	48%	70%				
6	Wendy Owen	63%	80%	51%				
7	Frank Waters	53%	85%	41%				
8	Barbara White	42%	63%	85%				
9								

Results / Sheet2 / Sheet3

Stage 3

We are now going to use some formulae to get the spreadsheet to do some calculations for us.

1. In cell E3 enter **Average**.

2. Cell E4 is the first cell where we want to enter the formula to AVERAGE cells B4, C4 and D4.

3. Copy the formula from cell E4 into E5 through to E8 to calculate the other averages.

4. Change the font style for cells A4 through to A8 to **Italics**.

5. Save your spreadsheet.

Your spreadsheet should now appear as shown on the top of the next page:

Stage 4

One more calculation is needed:

1. In cell A10 enter **Module Average** (in italics)

2. Widen column A so that the text in A10 fits within the column

3. Cell B10 is the first cell where we want to enter the formula to calculate the average of cells B4 through to B8.

4. Copy the formula from cell B10 into C10 and D10 to calculate the other averages

5. Underline B10, C10, D10

6. Save your spreadsheet.

The final spreadsheet is shown below.

You have now completed the first exercise.

Exercise 2 – using currencies and dates

In this exercise we will be working with more numerical data, utilising currencies and dates. The data relates to the summer sales of English novels by a bookshop.

Stage 1

This stage is to create our basic layout.

1.   Open a new workbook

2.   Move to Sheet2

3.   Change the name of the sheet to **Sales**

4.   In cell A1, enter **Summer sales**, (in bold text)

5.   In cell A3, enter **Date**, (underlined and bold)

6.   Enter **Book, Quantity, Value** in cells B3,C3,D3 respectively, (underlined and bold)

7.   Move the contents of A1 (Summer sales) to cell B1

8.   Merge cells B1 and C1

9.   Centre the text across B1 and C1

10.   Save the workbook with the name **T2Exercise2**

Your spreadsheet should look as shown in the image below:

Stage 2

We are now going to enter some data.

1. Enter the data below in the appropriate spreadsheet columns.

Date	Book	Quantity	Value
01/06/10	Lord of the Rings	10	100.34
05/06/10	Pride and Prejudice	5	45.80
16/06/10	Far from the Madding Crowd	8	65.75
23/06/10	Oliver Twist	3	22.75
03/07/10	Wuthering Heights	6	42.91
20/07/10	Pride and Prejudice	2	18.95
31/07/10	Lord of the Rings	2	22.45

2. Widen column B to enclose the longest piece of text

3. Format the Value column to use currency £ (with 2 decimal places)

4. Modify the format of all the dates to display the year as 2010 (ie four digits yyyy)

5. Save the workbook again with the name **T2Exercise2**

Your spreadsheet should look as shown in the screen below:

Stage 3

We need to make some modifications to the data.

1. We require a column for the author, insert a column between columns B and C.

2. Enter **Author** in cell C3 (bold and underline)

3. Enter the text for the Author column as shown in the table below, using the spelling provided.

Date	Book	Author	Quantity	Value
01/06/10	Lord of the Rings	Tolkien	10	100.34
05/06/10	Pride and Prejudice	Austin	5	45.80
16/06/10	Far from the Madding Crowd	Hardy	8	65.75
23/06/10	Oliver Twist	Dickens	3	22.75
03/07/10	Wuthering Heights	Bronte	6	42.91
20/07/10	Pride and Prejudice	Austin	2	18.95
31/07/10	Lord of the Rings	Tolkien	2	22.45

4. Adjust column C to the right width for the text.

5. A row is missing within July, insert a row between the row for 03/07/01 and 20/07/10.

6. Enter the data for the row from the table below.

Date	Book	Author	Quantity	Value
15/07/10	Oliver Twist	Dickens	2	16.45

7. Change the format for column C (Author) so that all text is aligned to the right of the cells.

8. The author 'Austin', should be spelt 'Austen', correct both occurrences.

9. Save your spreadsheet.

Your spreadsheet should appear as shown in the screen below:

	C13		f_x			
	A	B	C	D	E	
1		Summer sales				
2						
3	Date	Book	Author	Quantity	Value	
4	01/06/2010	Lord of the Rings	Tolkien	10	£100.34	
5	05/06/2010	Pride and Prejudice	Austen	5	£45.80	
6	16/06/2010	Far from the Madding Crowd	Hardy	8	£65.75	
7	23/06/2010	Oliver Twist	Dickens	3	£22.75	
8	03/07/2010	Wuthering Heights	Bronte	6	£42.91	
9	15/07/2010	Oliver Twist	Dickens	2	£16.45	
10	20/07/2010	Pride and Prejudice	Austen	2	£18.95	
11	31/07/2010	Lord of the Rings	Tolkien	2	£22.45	
12						

Sheet1 **Sales** Sheet3

Stage 4

In this stage, we will make some more changes to the format and enter some calculations.

1.   The text for the Value heading is aligned to the left and all the numeric values are aligned to the right. Align E3 text to the right.

2.   Change the font size of Summer sales to size 18 (cells B1 and C1)

3.   Increase the height of row 1 to allow for the larger font.

4.   Move the text of E3 (Value) to cell E2.

5.   Enter text **(£)** in cell E3 and centre in the cell.

6.   Enter text **Euros** in cell F3 and centre in the cell.

7.   Merge cells E2 and F2, and centre the text.

8.   We are going to use an exchange rate of 1 pound = 1.15 euros, and we are going to calculate the values of the sales in euros in column F. Enter a formula in cell F4 to calculate the value in euros (E4 * 1.15)

9.   Copy the formula from cell F4 to F5 through to F11

10.   Change the format of column F to Currency, euros.

11.   Save your spreadsheet.

Your spreadsheet should appear as shown in the screen below:

F4			fx =E4*1.15				
	A	B	C	D	E	F	
1		**Summer sales**					
2						Value	
3	Date	Book		Author	Quantity	(£)	Euros
4	01/06/2010	Lord of the Rings		Tolkien	10	£100.34	€ 115.39
5	05/06/2010	Pride and Prejudice		Austen	5	£45.80	€ 52.67
6	16/06/2010	Far from the Madding Crowd		Hardy	8	£65.75	€ 75.61
7	23/06/2010	Oliver Twist		Dickens	3	£22.75	€ 26.16
8	03/07/2010	Wuthering Heights		Bronte	6	£42.91	€ 49.35
9	15/07/2010	Oliver Twist		Dickens	2	£16.45	€ 18.92
10	20/07/2010	Pride and Prejudice		Austen	2	£18.95	€ 21.79
11	31/07/2010	Lord of the Rings		Tolkien	2	£22.45	€ 25.82

Sheet1   **Sales**   Sheet3

Save and close your spreadsheet package.

Exercise 3 – further formatting and use of formulas

In this exercise we are going to make further changes to the spreadsheet which we created in the previous exercise.

Stage 1

This stage involves changing formats and text alignment within our spreadsheet.

1.   Start the spreadsheet package and open the workbook file **T2Exercise2**

2.   The date in cell A10 is wrong and should read **21/07/2010**, edit the cell to make the change.

3.   Change the format of the dates in column A to give the month name rather than 2 numeric digits e.g. 01 June 2010

4.   Modify the width of column A if necessary.

5.   Align all the dates to the **left** of the cells.

6.   For those books which have made more than one sale (ie sales on more than one day), change the text of the book title (column B) to italics, (for example *Oliver Twist*).

7.   Save the workbook with the name **T2Exercise3**

Your spreadsheet should appear as shown in the screen below:

	A	B	C	D	E	F
	A12		f_x			
1		**Summer sales**				
2					**Value**	
3	**Date**	**Book**	**Author**	**Quantity**	**(£)**	**Euros**
4	01 June 2010	*Lord of the Rings*	Tolkien	10	£100.34	€ 115.39
5	05 June 2010	*Pride and Prejudice*	Austen	5	£45.80	€ 52.67
6	16 June 2010	Far from the Madding Crowd	Hardy	8	£65.75	€ 75.61
7	23 June 2010	*Oliver Twist*	Dickens	3	£22.75	€ 26.16
8	03 July 2010	Wuthering Heights	Bronte	6	£42.91	€ 49.35
9	15 July 2010	*Oliver Twist*	Dickens	2	£16.45	€ 18.92
10	21 July 2010	*Pride and Prejudice*	Austen	2	£18.95	€ 21.79
11	31 July 2010	*Lord of the Rings*	Tolkien	2	£22.45	€ 25.82

Sheet1 **Sales** Sheet3

Stage 2

This stage requires entry of some formulas.

1. We want to total the sales for the book 'Lord of the Rings'. Copy the book title for this book to cell B13.

2. Remove the style of Italics to change the text style to normal.

3. In cell C13, enter the text **Sales**.

4. In cell D13, enter a formula to add up only the quantity cells for this book.

5. In Row 14 repeat the steps 1 to 4 above for the book *Oliver Twist* to give total sales for this book.

6. Save the spreadsheet.

Your spreadsheet should look as shown in the image below.

	D13	▼	f_x =D4+D11				⊗
	A	B	C	D	E	F	
1		**Summer sales**					
2					Value		
3	Date	Book	Author	Quantity	(£)	Euros	
4	01 June 2010	*Lord of the Rings*	Tolkien	10	£100.34	€ 115.39	
5	05 June 2010	*Pride and Prejudice*	Austen	5	£45.80	€ 52.67	
6	16 June 2010	Far from the Madding Crowd	Hardy	8	£65.75	€ 75.61	
7	23 June 2010	*Oliver Twist*	Dickens	3	£22.75	€ 26.16	
8	03 July 2010	Wuthering Heights	Bronte	6	£42.91	€ 49.35	
9	15 July 2010	*Oliver Twist*	Dickens	2	£16.45	€ 18.92	
10	21 July 2010	*Pride and Prejudice*	Austen	2	£18.95	€ 21.79	
11	31 July 2010	*Lord of the Rings*	Tolkien	2	£22.45	€ 25.82	
12							
13		Lord of the Rings	Sales	12			
14		Oliver Twist	Sales	5			

Sheet1   **Sales**   Sheet3

Stage 3

This stage requires entry of some further formulas.

1. We are to calculate the price paid for each sale. In cell G3 Enter **Book Price**, widen column G accordingly.

2. We are going to calculate the price using the value in pounds and dividing by the quantity. Enter the formula in cell G4 to calculate the book price.

3. Copy the formula from G4 to cells G5 through to G11.

4. The quantity entered for 1st of June should be **11** not 10. Make the change, see how all calculations using this value automatically update.

5. Select all cells and change the font face to Arial, size 10.

6. Check all headings (text) in row 3 is bold and underlined.

7. Change the format of the Euros values to display no decimal places.

8. Save the spreadsheet.

Your spreadsheet should appear as shown in the image at the top of the next page.

	C16		fx				
	A	B	C	D	E	F	G
1		Summer sales					
2					Value		
3	Date	Book	Author	Quantity	(£)	Euros	Book Price
4	01 June 2010	Lord of the Rings	Tolkien	11	£100.34	€ 115	£9.12
5	05 June 2010	Pride and Prejudice	Austen	5	£45.80	€ 53	£9.16
6	16 June 2010	Far from the Madding Crowd	Hardy	8	£65.75	€ 76	£8.22
7	23 June 2010	Oliver Twist	Dickens	3	£22.75	€ 26	£7.58
8	03 July 2010	Wuthering Heights	Bronte	6	£42.91	€ 49	£7.15
9	15 July 2010	Oliver Twist	Dickens	2	£16.45	€ 19	£8.23
10	21 July 2010	Pride and Prejudice	Austen	2	£18.95	€ 22	£9.48
11	31 July 2010	Lord of the Rings	Tolkien	2	£22.45	€ 26	£11.23
12							
13		Lord of the Rings	Sales	13			
14		Oliver Twist	Sales	5			

Stage 4

In this stage we are going to look at how to print out the spreadsheet.

1. Select **Print Preview** from your menu. You will see that not all of our columns can be seen, and the Book Price column gets pushed on to a second page.

2. Select **Page Setup**, and change the setup so that the page will print Landscape.

3. We are now going to create a header which is to appear on our printed documents. Using your **Page Setup** options, enter the text **Confidential**, so that it will appear at the top and left of the document.

4. Now insert a footer, again using your **Page Setup** options put a page number to appear in the centre of the document.

    A final Print Preview should look like the image below:

				Value		
Confidential						
	Summer sales					
Date	Book	Author	Quantity	(£)	Euros	Book Price
01 June 2010	Lord of the Rings	Tolkien	11	£100.34	€ 115	£9.12
05 June 2010	Pride and Prejudice	Austen	5	£45.80	€ 53	£9.16
16 June 2010	Far from the Madding Crowd	Hardy	8	£65.75	€ 76	£8.22
23 June 2010	Oliver Twist	Dickens	3	£22.75	€ 26	£7.58
03 July 2010	Wuthering Heights	Bronte	6	£42.91	€ 49	£7.15
15 July 2010	Oliver Twist	Dickens	2	£16.45	€ 19	£8.23
21 July 2010	Pride and Prejudice	Austen	2	£18.95	€ 22	£9.48
31 July 2010	Lord of the Rings	Tolkien	2	£22.45	€ 26	£11.23
	Lord of the Rings	Sales	13			
	Oliver Twist	Sales	5			
	Page 1					

Note:

It is important to practise further with **Page Setup**, using **Fit to page**, setting up your own headers and footers, and utilising built-in options for dates and page numbers where possible.

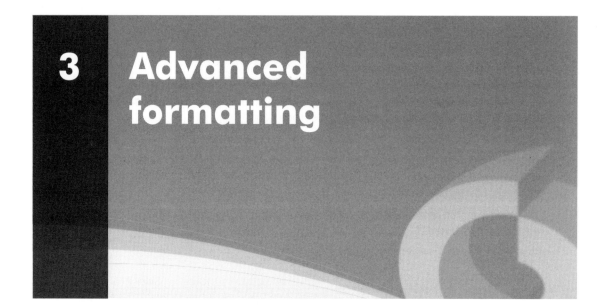

3 Advanced formatting

this chapter covers...

This chapter provides an introduction to advanced formatting for those new to spreadsheets. It explains and takes you through the basic concepts and techniques listed below. By the time you have finished this chapter and carried out the exercises which follow, you should be able to produce clearly formatted, easy-to-read spreadsheets. The concepts covered are:

- *cell display - borders, fill colours*

- *moving rows and columns*

- *hiding rows and columns*

- *specifying row height and column width*

- *cell and sheet protection*

- *conditional formatting*

- *data validation*

Note that the the step-by-step instructions given in this chapter are based on the Microsoft® Excel model, but the concepts and techniques described relate to all spreadsheet packages.

CELL DISPLAY

using borders

We sometimes want to make a cell or group of cells stand out within the spreadsheet.

One of the ways we can do this is to use **Borders**, which are just lines which we add around the edges of a cell or group of cells.

Borders can vary in colour and thickness; they can also be dotted or broken.

They can also be used to split groups of numbers to improve legibility by applying the border to just one edge of a cell.

To apply borders:

■ select all the required cells

■ right click on the selected cell or cells

■ select **Format cells**

■ select **Border**

■ choose the **Line style** and **Colour**

■ apply to the required edges using either preset borders

■ *or* clicking within the outline box to select edges (as shown in the screen illustration on the next page)

Number	Alignment	Font	Border	Fill	Protection

Line

Style:

None

Color:

Automatic

Presets

None   Outline   Inside

Border

Text   Text

using font and fill colour

It is possible to change both the colour of the **Font face** and the colour of the background within a cell, known as the **Fill colour**.

	A1			f_x	Bank transactions		
	A	B	C	D	E	F	G
1	Bank transactions						
2							
3	Opening balance	£1,500.00			Cell fill color grey		
4	Closing balance	£1,289.05			with a thin border		
5							
6	Date	Debit	Credit	Balance			
7	02/07/2010	£95.34	£0.00	£1,404.66			
8	11/07/2010	£0.00	£25.50	£1,430.16			
9	15/07/2010	£0.00	£34.78	£1,464.94			
10	22/07/2010	£67.90	£0.00	£1,397.04			
11	28/07/2010	£107.99	£0.00	£1,289.05			
12	Totals	£271.23	£60.28		£1,289.05		
13							

Sheet1 **July** Sheet3

To change the font colour:

- select all the required cells

- right click on the selected cell or cells

- select **Format cells**

- select **Font**

- choose the **Colour** you require

To set the cell Fill colour:

- select all the required cells

- right click on the selected cell or cells

- select **Format cells**

- select **Fill**

- choose the **Colour** you require

MOVING A COLUMN OR A ROW

Sometimes we may wish to change our basic layout and **move either a column or a row** within the layout.

For example, we might wish to move the Average column in an expenditure forecast to display before the months, as you can see in the image below:

	A13		f_x					
	A	B	C	D	E	F	G	H
1	Expenditure forecast							
2				*Average column moved to column B*				
3								
4		Average	January	February	March	April	May	June
5	Salaries	£85,000	£80,000	£80,000	£80,000	£90,000	£90,000	£90,000
6	Insurance	£333	£1,000	£500	£0	£0	£0	£500
7	Rent	£3,500	£3,500	£3,500	£3,500	£3,500	£3,500	£3,500
8	Accountancy	£135	£270	£0	£270	£0	£270	£0
9	Advertising	£550	£0	£1,500	£0	£0	£0	£1,800
10	Postage	£118	£95	£190	£95	£80	£95	£150
11	Stationery	£55	£57	£90	£0	£90	£0	£90

Alternatively. we might want to move the rows around so that the expenditure types are ordered alphabetically, as shown below.

	A13		f_x					
	A	B	C	D	E	F	G	H
1	Expenditure forecast							
2				*Expenditure types now ordered alphabetically*				
3								
4		Average	January	February	March	April	May	June
5	Accountancy	£135	£270	£0	£270	£0	£270	£0
6	Advertising	£550	£0	£1,500	£0	£0	£0	£1,800
7	Insurance	£333	£1,000	£500	£0	£0	£0	£500
8	Postage	£118	£95	£190	£95	£80	£95	£150
9	Rent	£3,500	£3,500	£3,500	£3,500	£3,500	£3,500	£3,500
10	Salaries	£85,000	£80,000	£80,000	£80,000	£90,000	£90,000	£90,000
11	Stationery	£55	£57	£90	£0	£90	£0	£90

To move a row:

■ right click on the row header of the row to move

■ select **Cut**

■ right click on the row header to where you want to move the row

■ select **Insert cut cells**

or

■ insert a row in the position that you want to move the row to

■ right click on the row header of the row to move

■ drag the row to the blank row and release

To move a column:

■ right click on the column header of the column to move

■ select **Cut**

■ right click on the column header where you to move the column to

■ select **Insert cut cells**

or

■ insert a column in the position that you want to move the column to

■ right click on the column header of the column to move

■ drag the column to the blank column and release

HIDE A ROW OR A COLUMN

Sometimes we may wish to **hide** certain data or calculations used in a spreadsheet from public view, for example salary data.

The **Hide row** or **column** option allows us to do this and still make use of the data within our spreadsheet.

In the spreadsheet on the next page Column D has been hidden.

To hide a row:

- right click on the row header

- select **Hide**

To hide a column:

- right click on the column header

- select **Hide**

It is also possible to unhide a row or column to make modifications.

To unhide a row:

- select the row headers of the rows either side of the hidden row

- select **Format**

- select **Unhide**

To unhide a column:

- select the column headers of the columns either side of the hidden column

- select **Format**

- select **Unhide**

SPECIFYING ROW HEIGHT AND COLUMN WIDTH

There are several ways of setting the **height of a row**, or **width of a column**. So far in this chapter we have looked at dragging the boundaries of the row or column to set the size.

For **columns**, it is also possible to specify the size as a number from 0 to 255 which represents the number of characters that can be displayed in a cell that is formatted with the standard font.

With a column width of zero, the column will be hidden.

For **rows**, it is possible to specify the size as a number from 0 to 409, which represents the height measurement in points (1 point equals approximately 1/72 inch or 0.35mm).

If the row height is set to zero, the row is hidden.

To set a column to a specific width:

■ select the column or columns that you want to change

■ from the menu options, select **Format column width**

■ enter the required value

	A	B	C	E	F	G	H	I	J
1	Bank transactions								
2									
3	Opening balance	£1,500.00							
4	Closing balance	£1,289.05							
5									
6	Date	Debit	Credit						
7	02/07/2010	£95.34	£0.00						
8	11/07/2010	£0.00	£25.50						
9	15/07/2010	£0.00	£34.78						
10	22/07/2010	£67.90	£0.00						
11	28/07/2010	£107.99	£0.00						
12	Totals	£271.23	£60.28	£1,289.05					
13									
14									
15									
16									

Column Width

Column width: 9

OK   Cancel

To set a row to a specific height:

■ select the row or rows that you want to change

■ from the menu options, select **Format row height**

■ enter the required value (see the screen on the next page)

CELL AND WORKSHEET PROTECTION

It can be important that the values within certain cells do not get changed by a user, for example a formula.

To prevent a cell being changed we can **lock** it. The default setting for a cell is usually locked. Locking a cell has no effect until the **worksheet** (also know as a '**sheet**') containing the cell is **protected**. If a user tries to change a locked cell on a protected worksheet he/she will get a message to the effect that the cell is protected and therefore read-only.

To lock a cell or cells:

■ select all the required cells

■ right click on the selected cell or cells

■ select **Format cells**

■ click the **Protection** tab

■ check the **Locked** box (see the screen below)

If locking a cell is to have any effect the worksheet containing the locked cells **must be protected**.

To protect a worksheet:

■ select the sheetname tab of the required worksheet

■ select **Protect sheet** from the menu bar

■ enter a memorable password as requested

It is very important to keep a note of the password, because if you lose a password, **you cannot recover it**. Without the necessary password all changes to protected cells would not be permitted, even by the creator of the worksheet.

If you do have the password and wish to change cells you first need to **unprotect the sheet**:

■ select the sheetname tab of the required worksheet

■ select **Unprotect sheet** from the menu bar

■ enter the password as requested

CONDITIONAL FORMATTING

We have covered the concepts of displaying cells with different fill colours and text colours, by selecting and changing.

Sometimes we may want a cell to change colour or display a different font face automatically depending on the value it may hold; this is known as **conditional formatting**.

This is especially useful if we have a large amount of data, where it would be easy to miss seeing certain values.

Conditional formatting allows you to define a rule or rules, and if the data meets the rules (conditions), it will display in the format that you have specified, in a different font or fill colour.

For example we may want all values less than £1,000 on a financial worksheet to be displayed in red text, so that they stand out.

Rules can be defined using a choice of arithmetic operators such as **greater than, less than, equal to, not equal to** and so on.

You can define more than one rule, and each rule can have several conditions within it.

In the example below we have applied formatting to the Postage costs in Row 9. The result of this will be that all cells where Postage costs are greater than £100 will fill with a grey background.

	A	B	C	D	E	F	G	H
	A13	▾	*fx*					
1	Expenditure forecast							
2								
3		January	February	March	April	May	June	Average
4	Salaries	£80,000	£80,000	£80,000	£90,000	£90,000	£90,000	
5	Insurance	£1,000	£500	£0	£0	£0	£500	
6	Rent	£3,500	£3,500	£3,500	£3,500	£3,500	£3,500	
7	Accountancy	£270	£0	£270	£0	£270	£0	
8	Advertising	£0	£1,500	£0	£0	£0	£1,800	
9	Postage	£95	£190	£95	£80	£95	£150	
10	Stationery	£57	£90	£0	£90	£0	£90	
11	Totals	£84,922	£85,780	£83,865	£93,670	£93,865	£96,040	
12								
13				Values exceed £100				

Sheet1   Sheet2   **Sheet3**

To set conditional formatting for a group of cells:

■ select the required cells

■ select **Conditional formatting** from the menu bar

■ enter the rule which you want to apply using the drop down list of 'greater than, less than, equal to' etc, and the required value

■ select the **Font style** and **Colour**, together with the fill colour and any other effects

DATA VALIDATION

When a spreadsheet is being used, it is possible we may only want to allow certain values in a particular cell; this might be to prevent data entry errors such as misspelling or to ensure consistency across the data.

It is possible to restrict the type of data which may be entered, such as a date, a whole number, or to provide a list of acceptable values, which will then be displayed as a drop down list when the user moves to the cell. This restriction of values is called **data validation**.

In the image on the next page we have restricted the values allowed in cells in the month column (column A) to three character month names. When you move to one of these cells, a drop down list appears showing the acceptable choices. You are only allowed to select from this list.

A6	▼		*fx*			
	A	B	C	D	E	F
1	**Sales**					
2						
3	**Month**	**Product**	**Value**			
4	Feb	Clothing	£1,500.00			
5	Feb	Jewellery	£220.00			
6		▼				
7	Jan / Feb	▲				
8	Mar	▬				
9	Apr / May					
10	Jun					
11	Jul / Aug	▼				

In the image below you can see that the choice of Product has also been restricted to allow only four specific values. When you select any of the cells in the product column the drop down list of products is displayed and you can choose from this list.

B6	▼		*fx*			
	A	B	C	D	E	F
1	**Sales**					
2						
3	**Month**	**Product**	**Value**			
4	Feb	Clothing	£1,500.00			
5	Feb	Jewellery	£220.00			
6	Mar	▼				
7		Accessories / Clothing				
8		Footwear				
9		Jewellery / Other				
10						

To define the data validation for a group of cells:

■ select the required cells

■ select **Data validation** from the menu bar

■ select the validation criteria from the drop down list (as seen in the screen on the next page)

■ if you select **List**, enter the values you want to allow, separated by commas

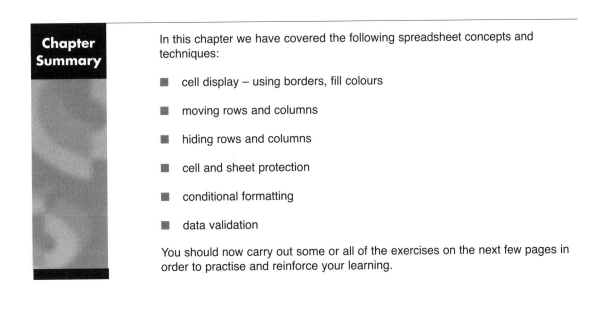

a note on copying data validation

Once you have formatted a cell with data validation, if you want to apply that same validation to another cell or cells, you can use normal **Copy** and **Paste** facilities and the data validation will apply to the cells where you paste.

Chapter Summary

In this chapter we have covered the following spreadsheet concepts and techniques:

■ cell display – using borders, fill colours

■ moving rows and columns

■ hiding rows and columns

■ cell and sheet protection

■ conditional formatting

■ data validation

You should now carry out some or all of the exercises on the next few pages in order to practise and reinforce your learning.

Activities

Exercise 1 – formatting, including data validation and presentation

In this first exercise we will create a simple time recording spreadsheet to record details of time spent on client work by a firm of accountants.

Stage 1

In this stage we create the basic layout of our spreadsheet. All text should be entered in the default typeface, font size 10, normal style.

1. Open a new workbook

2. Move to Sheet1

3. Change the name of the sheet to **Time record**

4. Move to cell A1, enter **Client work log**

5. Move to cell A3, enter **Name**

6. Format cell B3 so that it has a thin solid black border all the way round, and is filled with a light grey.

7. In cell A4 enter **Department**

8. Format cell B4 so that it has a thin solid black border all the way round, and is filled with a light grey.

9. In cell A5 enter **Month**

10. Move to cell B5, apply data validation to the cell, to allow the user to pick the name of the month from a list of 3 character month names, ie Jan, Feb, Mar, and so on for the whole year, displayed in calendar order.

11. Format cell B5 so that it has a thin solid black border all the way round, and is filled with a light grey.

12. Widen column A to ensure all text is enclosed within it.

13. Widen column B to allow enough space for a full name.

14. Save the workbook with the name **T3Exercise1**

Your spreadsheet should appear as shown in the screen at the top of the next page:

Stage 2

We will continue creating the basic template for entry of client time recording information.

1. In cell A7, enter **Date**

2. In cell B7, enter **Client**

3. In cell C7, enter **Hours**

4. Column A is where we are going to enter date information, so format this column to display dates in the form dd/mm/yy (eg 14/03/01)

5. For the hours column we will restrict the entry to only allow whole or half hours. Apply data validation to cell C8, giving a list of values from 0.5 through to 4.0, ie 0.5,1.0,1.5, etc

6. To apply the same data validation to C9 through to C30, copy cell C8 to cells C9 through to C30

7. Merge cells A1, B1, C1 and centre the text 'Client work log' across the three cells.

8. Save your spreadsheet (keeping the same name – **T3Exercise1**)

Your spreadsheet should appear as shown in the screen below:

Stage 3

We will now use borders to improve the spreadsheet presentation. All borders should be a thin solid black border unless otherwise specified.

1. Apply a border to the top and bottom edges of A7 through to C7

2. Apply a border to the left and right edges of C7 through to C30

3. Apply a border to the lower edge of A30 through to C30

4. Apply a border to the left and right edges of A7 through to A30

5. Insert a column before column A

6. Set the width of column A to 4

7. Save your spreadsheet (keeping the same name – **T3Exercise1**)

Your spreadsheet should appear as shown in the screen below.

Stage 4

We are now going to complete the formatting and leave the sheet ready to be used for data entry.

1. Insert 2 rows above row 7

2. In cell C7 enter **Total**

3. In cell D7 enter the formula to add cells D10 through to D32

4. Format D7 to display with one decimal place and with a bold font

5. Put a double line border on the bottom edge of cells C7 and D7

6. Make rows 2, 6, and 8 height 6

7. Lock all cells with text or values already in.

8. Unlock cells C3, C4, C5, B10 through B32, C10 through C32, D10 through D32

9. Protect the sheet with password **ex3**

10. Save your spreadsheet.

Your spreadsheet should appear as shown in the screen below.

Exercise 2 – modifying spreadsheet presentation

In this exercise we will take an existing spreadsheet and modify it to improve the presentation and legibility.

Stage 1

This stage covers the processes of locating and opening a previously created workbook.

1. The workbook file can be downloaded from www.osbornebooks.co.uk ('Resources') filename **T3modules**

2. Save the workbook as **T3Exercise2**

    The workbook is shown below.

	A	B	C	D	E	F	G	H
1	Midterm exams							
2								
3	Name	Module1	Module2	Module3	Average			
4	John Smith	75%	62%	45%	61%			
5	Peter Jones	61%	48%	70%	60%			
6	Wendy Owen	63%	80%	51%	65%			
7	Frank Waters	53%	85%	41%	60%			
8	Barbara White	42%	63%	85%	63%			
9								
10	Module Average	59%	68%	58%				
11								
12								

Results / Sheet2 / Sheet3

Stage 2

Now we have got the workbook open with the new name, we will make some changes to the format.

1. Move (re-arrange) the results rows (rows 4 to 8) so that they are in alphabetical order by surname.

2. Move the average column so that it is after the Name column and before the Module1 column.

3. The mark for Barbara White Module 3 should be **45%** not 85%. Make the correction.

4. Format the average column to display as a percentage with 2 decimal places.

5. Apply conditional formatting to the average column (column B), so that values greater than 60% are shown in bold with a grey fill.

6. Apply conditional formatting to all of the Module percentages (columns C, D, E) so that those marks less than 50% are displayed in a white font on a black fill background.

7. Save the workbook with the name **T3Exercise2**

    Your spreadsheet should appear as shown in the screen below.

	A	B	C	D	E
	A11			f_x	
2					
3	**Name**	**Average**	**Module1**	**Module2**	**Module3**
4	Peter Jones	59.67%	61%	48%	70%
5	Wendy Owen	**64.67%**	63%	80%	51%
6	John Smith	**60.67%**	75%	62%	45%
7	Frank Waters	59.67%	53%	85%	41%
8	Barbara White	50.00%	42%	63%	45%
9					
10	Module Average		59%	68%	50%
11					

Results   Sheet2   Sheet3

Exercise 3 – data validation and worksheet protection

In this exercise we are again going to create a spreadsheet containing sales agents' details. The spreadsheet will utilise data validation.

Stage 1

We are going to create the basic template for entry of sales agents' details.

1. Open a new workbook.

2. Enter the heading *Agent details* in cell A1, font size 16, style italics

3. Enter **Name, Country, Active, Quantity, Rate(£), Value** in cells A3 through to F3 respectively, make this text bold and underlined.

4. Allowable values for Country are **UK, USA, FR, IT, GER**. Apply data validation to cells B4 through to B20 to restrict entry to these values.

5. Allowable values for Active are **Y, N**. Apply data validation to cells C4 through to C20 to restrict entry to these values.

6. Extend column A to width 30 characters.

7. Save the workbook with the name **T3Exercise3**

Your spreadsheet should appear as shown in the screen below.

Stage 2

We are now going to enter some data.

1. Enter the data from the table below into the appropriate worksheet columns, Note that in this exercise the column heading 'Rate(£)' refers to the commission rate of the agent and the heading 'Value' is the payment due to the agent.

Name	Country	Active	Quantity	Rate(£)
Jason White	UK	Y	150	£22.00
Peter Lighthouse	FR	N	200	£20.00
Joan Brown	FR	Y	58	£30.00
Karen Parker	IT	Y	85	£26.00
Sammy Smith	USA	N	235	£12.00
George Warner	GER	Y	124	£19.00

2. Enter a formula in column F to calculate the value (payment due) for each agent (Quantity * Rate(£)). Use Copy and Paste where possible.

3. Display values in the Value column (column F) as currency £ with no decimal places.

4. Align the column headings 'Quantity, Rate(£), Value' to the right. (Cells D3, E3, F3)

5. Save the workbook with the same name (**T3Exercise3**)

    Your spreadsheet should appear as shown in the screen below.

	A	B	C	D	E	F
	A12			f_x		
1	*Agent details*					
2						
3	Name	Country	Active	Quantity	Rate(£)	Value
4	Jason White	UK	Y	150	£22.00	£3,300
5	Peter Lighthouse	FR	N	200	£20.00	£4,000
6	Joan Brown	FR	Y	58	£30.00	£1,740
7	Karen Parker	IT	Y	85	£26.00	£2,210
8	Sammy Smith	USA	N	235	£12.00	£2,820
9	George Warner	GER	Y	124	£19.00	£2,356
10						
11						
12						

Sheet1 / Sheet2 / Sheet3

Stage 3

We will now protect the worksheet.

1. Lock all those cells containing heading text or a formula.

2. Unlock all those cells where data is going to be entered in columns A, B, C, D, E and F.

3. Protect the sheet, with password **ex3**

4. Enter details for another agent as shown below.

Name	Country	Active	Quantity	Rate(£)
Trevor Black	UK	Y	175	£23.00

5. Copy the formula to calculate the Value cell for this agent

6. Save your spreadsheet.

Your spreadsheet should appear as shown in the screen below.

	A	B	C	D	E	F
1	Agent details					
2						
3	Name	Country	Active	Quantity	Rate(£)	Value
4	Jason White	UK	Y	150	£22.00	£3,300
5	Peter Lighthouse	FR	N	200	£20.00	£4,000
6	Joan Brown	FR	Y	58	£30.00	£1,740
7	Karen Parker	IT	Y	85	£26.00	£2,210
8	Sammy Smith	USA	N	235	£12.00	£2,820
9	George Warner	GER	Y	124	£19.00	£2,356
10	Trevor Black	UK	Y	175	£23.00	£4,025
11						
12						

Cell reference: A11

Sheet1 / Sheet2 / Sheet3

Stage 4

We will now adjust the formatting and leave the sheet ready to be circulated.

1. Unprotect the sheet

2. Hide the Quantity and Rate columns (columns D and E)

3. Hide the row for Joan Brown (row 6)

4. Protect the sheet, with password **ex3**

5. Save your spreadsheet.

    The final spreadsheet is shown below.

	A	B	C	F	G	H
1	*Agent details*					
2						
3	<u>Name</u>	<u>Country</u>	<u>Active</u>	<u>Value</u>		
4	Jason White	UK	Y	£3,300		
5	Peter Lighthouse	FR	N	£4,000		
7	Karen Parker	IT	Y	£2,210		
8	Sammy Smith	USA	N	£2,820		
9	George Warner	GER	Y	£2,356		
10	Trevor Black	UK	Y	£4,025		
11						
12						

Sheet1 Sheet2 Sheet3

4 Spreadsheet functions

this chapter covers...

This chapter covers the creation of formulas, and shows how you can make use of some of the built-in calculation facilities provided by spreadsheet software. It explains and takes you through the concepts and techniques listed below. By the time you have finished this chapter and carried out the exercises which follow, you should be able to produce spreadsheets which perform a variety of calculations. The concepts and techniques covered are:

- *formulas*

- *mathematical operators*

- *functions*

- *ranges*

- *mathematical functions*

- *cell addressing*

- *date functions*

- *logical functions and operators*

- *lookup functions*

- *circular references in formulas*

Note that the the step-by-step instructions given in this chapter are based on the Microsoft® Excel model, but the concepts and techniques described relate to all spreadsheet packages.

FORMULAS

As we have seen in previous chapters, whenever we wish to carry out a calculation or enter a formula into a cell within our spreadsheet, we move to the cell where we want the formula to appear and start by entering an equal sign =.

The formula can take a very simple form, containing just numbers, or a mixture of numbers and cell references, or as we have seen earlier, a function and cell references.

Examples of formulas include:

=3 + 2

=D6 – 1.15

=D6 * D7

=D32

Note that as we create the formula, any spaces we insert within the formula are automatically ignored.

One of the most significant points about formulas which has already been mentioned, is that when we copy a formula from one cell to another cell or group of cells, the row and column numbers automatically change as appropriate. they will automatically relate to the row or column references of the new cell to which the formula has been copied.

MATHEMATICAL OPERATORS

The common mathematical operators which we will use in our formulas are as follows:-

■ Addition: +

■ Subtraction: –

■ Multiplication: *

■ Division: /

We also make use of brackets: ( )

As with our normal mathematics there is an **order** that will be followed when a formula is interpreted, known as the **operator precedence**.

The order of calculations within any formula is as follows:

■ any calculation contained in brackets is done first

■ division and multiplication are ranked the same

■ addition and subtraction are ranked the same

So, if we want to group parts of our calculation to ensure that certain parts are calculated before a subsequent part, then we would use brackets.

For example:

$$= (B3 + 5)/100$$

Here 5 is added to B3 and the result is divided by 100.

This gives a different result to

$$= B3+5/100$$

Here 5 is divided by 100 and the result is added to B3

As you can see brackets play a very important part in our construction of formulas.

FUNCTIONS – AN EXPLANATION

Spreadsheet packages contain built-in formulas called **Functions** that make it easy to perform common calculations on data. For example, **=SUM( )** is a function which can be used to add up values, as we have seen in the earlier chapters of this book.

Most functions are designed to accept data which is then used in the calculations. This data is entered within the round brackets which follow the function's name.

For example, **=SUM(A1,A2,A3)** is a formula which uses the SUM function to add up the values of the three cells.

These values are also known as '**arguments**'.

As you can see, each argument (or value) is usually separated from the previous argument (value) by a comma.

The **type** of argument will vary from function to function: it could be a number, or a cell reference, or group of cells.

The **number** of arguments may also vary from function to function.

The most common forms of argument are a cell reference, or group of cell references, as we shall see in the examples which follow. Look at cell A1 in the screen at the top of the next page.

As you can see in this screen, the SUM function is prompting the user to enter the first argument or number to be added. This could be a cell reference or an actual number.

If an argument is **optional** (ie you don't have to enter it) you will see the argument in square brackets, for example [number2], as shown above.

The result which a function creates is said to be the value **returned** by the function, and is known as the **return** value.

RANGES

A range is a **group or block of cells in a worksheet**. It is essentially a shorthand way of specifying the first and last cell and automatically including all the cells in between.

A range is identified by the cell reference of the first cell (upper left cell), followed by a colon, then the cell reference of the last cell (bottom right).

Examples of a range of cells include:

> D4:D11   – all the cells are in the same column
>
> C4:F4   – all the cells are in the same row
>
> D4:F10   – a block of cells across several rows and columns

A range of cells as described above can be used as an argument within a function, for example =SUM(D4:D11).

MATHEMATICAL FUNCTIONS

The functions we are going to cover in this section are as follows:

■ ABS

■ INT

■ SUM

We are also going to explain the AUTOSUM facility, which is available to help create formulas within Microsoft Excel.

ABS

The ABS function 'returns' the **absolute value** of a number, which is the value of a number **without its sign**:

=ABS(number)

The ABS function has just one argument:

■ a number is required

For example:

=ABS(-2) . . . means that the number's sign will be removed and will return the value 2

=ABS(2) . . . will also return the value 2

INT

The INT function rounds a number down to the integer (ie whole number):

=INT(number)

The INT function has just one argument:

■ the number may contain decimals which you wish to round down to an integer

For example: =INT(2.45) would return the value 2

=INT(2.99) would also return the value 2

SUM

We have already used the SUM function in this book. The SUM function adds all the numbers that you specify as arguments. Each argument can be a number, a cell reference, a range of cells, or the result of another function:

=SUM(number1, [number2], [number3],...)

The SUM function has these arguments:

■   number1 is required

■   number2, number3 . . .   are optional

You can specify up to a total of 255 arguments (values) to be added together. For example:

=SUM(C2,C16,C20)

This would return the sum of the numbers in the cells C2, C16, and C20.

The screen illustrated below adds the values for the 'odd' numbered weeks for Smiths Ltd, using =SUM(B4, D4, F4), producing a total value of 45.

	G4		f_x	=SUM(B4,D4,F4)			
	A	B	C	D	E	F	G
1	Work bookings						
2							
3	Client	Week1	Week2	Week3	Week4	Week5	Odd weeks
4	Smiths Ltd	15	15	15	15	15	45
5	Jones and Partner	12	8	10	9	9	
6	Redwoods	13	20	11	7	8	
7	Underhills	13	20	11	2	9	
8							
9							

Time data Sheet2 Sheet3

SUM is often used for a **range of cells**, for example:

=SUM(C2:C16)

This would return the sum of all the numbers in the range C2 to C16, ie cells C2,C3,C4,C5 etc... all the way to C16.

The screen illustrated below uses the formula =SUM(B4:F4,50) to total all five weeks for Smiths Ltd and add a value of 50. This produces a total of 125.

	G4		f_x	=SUM(B4:F4,50)			
	A	B	C	D	E	F	G
1	Work bookings						
2							
3	Client	Week1	Week2	Week3	Week4	Week5	Forecast
4	Smiths Ltd	15	15	15	15	15	125
5	Jones and Partner	12	8	10	9	9	
6	Redwoods	13	20	11	7	8	
7	Underhills	13	20	11	2	9	
8							
9							

Time data Sheet2 Sheet3

AUTOSUM

This is a facility available in Microsoft Excel, which may not be available in other spreadsheet packages. It provides a quick way of selecting ranges of cells, usually for totalling, without having to manually specify or select the start and end cells for the range.

You select the cell where you want to position a total, and AUTOSUM will guess which cells above, or to the left you want to add up.

	A	B	C	D	E	F	G
2							
3	Client	Week1	Week2	Week3	Week4	Week5	Average
4	Smiths Ltd	15	15	15	15	15	15
5	Jones and Partner	12	8	10	9	9	10.33333333
6	Redwoods	13	20	11	7	8	
7	Underhills	13	20	11	2	9	55
8		=SUM(B4:B7)					
9		SUM(number1, [number2], ...)					
10							

COUNT   ✗ ✓ f_x =SUM(B4:B7)

Time data   Sheet2   Sheet3

In the example above, we have selected cell B8, then selected AUTOSUM from the menu bar. You can see that the formula =SUM(B4:B7) is automatically shown in the cell. If you just press **RETURN** this formula will be entered into the cell.

how to use AUTOSUM

■   select a cell below the column of numbers or to the right of the row of numbers

■   select AUTOSUM from the menu bar; a dotted rectangle will be displayed, highlighting the numbers to be included

■   if the appropriate cells are included, press **RETURN**

■   if not, use the mouse to drag the boundaries of the rectangle to include the appropriate cells.

CELL ADDRESSING

The way in which a cell is referenced is known as its address, for example A12, B49. This becomes important when we are using formulas. We have two ways of referencing cells within formulas:

■   relative addressing

■   absolute addressing

relative addressing

As we have seen, when we copy a formula from one cell to another, the formula is automatically adjusted to reflect the row or column of the new cell. This is called **relative addressing**: the formula is adjusted relative to the new cell.

We have seen that if you copy the formula

=SUM(B3:E3)

down a row from cell F3 to cell F4, the formula becomes

=SUM(B4:E4)

Similarly, for columns if you copy the formula

=SUM(B4:B8)

from cell B9 across a column to cell C9, the formula becomes

= SUM(C4:C8)

absolute addressing

Sometimes we do not want the cell reference to change as we copy a formula – we want to keep a reference to an original cell or cells. To do this we use the dollar sign: $.

For example, $B$3 would refer to cell B3, and, when placed in a formula and copied, the copies would all also refer to B3.

In the example below we have entered an hourly rate in cell B3, which we wish to apply to all the totals. We have created a formula in cell G6 to give us a monetary value for the work carried out for the client using the formula:

=F6 * B3

	COUNT	▾	× ✓ fx	=F6*B3				≫
	A	B	C	D	E	F	G	
1	Work bookings							
2								
3	Hourly rate	£20						
4								
5	Client	Week1	Week2	Week3	Week4	Total	Value	
6	Smiths Ltd	15	15	15	15	60	=F6*B3	
7	Jones and Partner	12	8	10	9	39		
8	Redwoods	13	20	11	7	51		
9	Underhills	13	20	11	2	46		
10		53						
11								
	◄ ◄ ► ►│ Time data / Sheet2 / Sheet3 / 💬							

We will now change the formula to =F6*$B$3 so that we can copy it and still keep the reference to B3, the cell where the hourly rate of £20 is entered.

	G6			f_x	=F6*$B$3			
	A	B	C	D	E	F	G	
1	Work bookings							
2								
3	Hourly rate	£20						
4								
5	Client	Week1	Week2	Week3	Week4	Total	Value	
6	Smiths Ltd	15	15	15	15	60	£1,200	
7	Jones and Partner	12	8	10	9	39		
8	Redwoods	13	20	11	7	51		
9	Underhills	13	20	11	2	46		
10		53						

When the formula =F6*$B$3 is then copied to cell G7, you can see on the screen image below that the cell reference has not changed, but remains B3. If the hourly rate changes from £20 to £22, then all you need to do is amend the amount entered in cell B3.

	G7			f_x	=F7*$B$3			
	A	B	C	D	E	F	G	
1	Work bookings							
2								
3	Hourly rate	£20						
4								
5	Client	Week1	Week2	Week3	Week4	Total	Value	
6	Smiths Ltd	15	15	15	15	60	£1,200	
7	Jones and Partner	12	8	10	9	39	£780	
8	Redwoods	13	20	11	7	51		
9	Underhills	13	20	11	2	46		
10		53						

Absolute cell addressing is a very important part of creating formulas within spreadsheets.

DATE FUNCTIONS

We often want to include date information in a spreadsheet, and we may want to perform a calculation on the information. For example, in a purchasing department, we might want a spreadsheet to display the expected interval of time between an order being placed with a supplier and the delivery date of the goods.

To enable date-based calculations, a spreadsheet stores all dates as numbers, based on the number of days from 1/1/1900. This is referred to as a **serial number** representation.

The time element of the date/time is also stored numerically as the decimal part of the serial number, for example the serial number 0.5 represents 12:00 noon.

You can see dates displayed as serial numbers, if you enter a date in a cell and the cell is not formatted as a date.

The functions we are going to cover in this section are as follows: **today** and **now**.

TODAY

The **TODAY** function returns the serial number of today's date based on your computer system clock, it does not include the time. The function is:

=TODAY( )

The TODAY function has no arguments (values).

For example, the formula:

= TODAY( ) +14

This would return the current date plus 14 days.

The =TODAY( ) function is useful if you want to have the current date displayed on a worksheet.

Another use would be if you wished to calculate a person's age as of today and you only had their date of birth.

In the example below, we have placed today's date in cell F1. This will change every time we re-open this workbook.

	F1	▼	fx	=TODAY()		¥
	A	B	C	D	E	F	G
1	Work bookings					19/10/2010	
2							
3	Hourly rate	£20					
4							
5	Client	Week1	Week2	Week3	Week4	Total	Value
6	Smiths Ltd	15	15	15	15	60	£1,200
7	Jones and Partner	12	8	10	9	39	
8	Redwoods	13	20	11	7	51	
9	Underhills	13	20	11	2	46	
10		53					
11							

H ◀ ▶ H   **Time data**   Sheet2   Sheet3   ↩

In some instances the result may appear as the serial number. If this happens, change the cell format to be date (see page 38) and it will display correctly.

NOW

The **NOW** function returns the serial number of today's date and the current time based on your computer system clock: =NOW ( )

The =NOW( ) function has no arguments (values).

In the example below, we have used the =NOW( ) function in cell F1. The time will change every time the worksheet re-calculates or is re-opened.

F1			f_x	=NOW()			
	A	B	C	D	E	Formula Bar F	G
1	Work bookings					19/10/2010 13:03	
2							
3	Hourly rate	£20					
4							
5	Client	Week1	Week2	Week3	Week4	Total	Value
6	Smiths Ltd	15	15	15	15	60	
7	Jones and Partner	12	8	10	9	39	
8	Redwoods	13	20	11	7	51	
9	Underhills	13	20	11	2	46	
10		53					
11							

Time data / Sheet2 / Sheet3

In some instances the result may appear as the serial number. If this happens,

■ change the cell format to be **Custom**

■ select format type dd/mm/yyyy hh:mm

and it will display correctly.

LOGICAL FUNCTIONS AND OPERATORS

A concept used regularly in spreadsheets is **conditional logic**.

This is a concept where if something is true, then something else happens.

For example:

> *if I swim in the sea **then** I will get wet*
>
> *if I do no work **then** I will not pass my exams*

Within the spreadsheet environment, we often want to test a cell for a certain value, and

■ if it is this value we make one thing happen

■ if it is not this value, we want something different to happen

logical operators

We can apply the standard comparison 'operators' to create situations where **conditional logic** can be used. These include:

- equal to (=)

- greater than (>)

- greater than or equal to (>=)

- less than (<)

- less than or equal to(<=)

- not equal to (<>)

For example, a condition could be that cell B10 is greater than 100 which we would express as:

B10>100

The main logical function which is used in spreadsheets is the **IF**( ) function

I F

The **IF** function returns one value if the condition you specify evaluates to TRUE, and another value if that condition evaluates to FALSE.

For example if you take an exam and the pass mark is 55%, if you get 60% you will pass, and if you get 54% you will fail.

Using the IF function you can use a spreadsheet to work out the 'pass' or' fail' for you, as we will see in the example on the next page.

The IF function is made up of three parts:

=IF(logical test, value if true, value if false)

These three parts can be explained as follows:

- **logical test**

  This can be any value or expression which can be evaluated to TRUE or FALSE. In the case of the exam pass mark this is

  =IF(F4>=55% . . . the logical test here is whether the mark in cell F4 is greater than or equal to 55%

- **value if true**

  This is the value which will be returned by the function if the condition evaluates to TRUE . . . if the value is 60% the answer is "PASS"

- **value if false**

  This is the value which will be returned by the function if the condition evaluates to FALSE . . . if the value is 54% (ie less than the pass mark of 55%,) the answer is "FAIL".

Therefore, to recap, the structure of the IF function is as follows:

=IF(logical test, value if true, value if false)

In the example we used to work out exam success or failure on the basis of a 55% pass mark, the IF function will be expressed as follows:

=IF(F4>=55%,"PASS","FAIL")

Note that:

■ any text which is to appear in the spreadsheet should be shown in quotes: **"PASS"**

■ the third part of the function - ie 'value if false' is optional; if it is not included, no value will be returned if the condition is false

In the example screen below, we have entered formulas in column G, for each person.

The formula in cell G4 for John Smith is:-

=IF(F4>=55%,"PASS","FAIL")

This formula looks at the value in cell F4, and since it more than 55%, this returns a value of PASS in cell G4.

Similarly for Peter Jones, the formula in cell G5 is:

=IF(F5>=55%,"PASS","FAIL")

This formula returns a value of FAIL because Peter Jones' average is less than 55%.

	G4			f_x	=IF(F4>=55%,"PASS","FAIL")		
	A	B	C	D	E	F	G
1	Midterm exams						
2							
3	**Name**	**Module1**	**Module2**	**Module3**	**Module4**	**Average**	
4	*John Smith*	75%	62%	45%	65%	61.75%	PASS
5	*Peter Jones*	61%	48%			54.50%	FAIL
6	*Wendy Owen*	63%	80%	51%	41%	58.75%	PASS
7	*Frank Waters*	53%		41%	64%	52.67%	FAIL
8	*Barbara White*	42%	63%	85%	43%	58.25%	PASS
9							
10	*Min*	42%	48%	41%	41%		
11							

Results / Sheet2 / Sheet3

It is a good idea to spend time to familiarise yourself with the IF function. It is used a great deal within spreadsheets and is very powerful.

LOOKUP FUNCTIONS

We can often have large amounts of data within a spreadsheet, and it may not be very easy to find a particular value, so we may wish to use an automated function to do it for us.

There are two built in functions which are regularly used: **HLOOKUP** and **VLOOKUP**.

HLOOKUP

The H in HLOOKUP is to identify that the function searches in a horizontal direction, ie along rows.

The function searches for a value in a particular row, and if found, it returns the matching value in the same column, from a specified row below the row being searched..

=HLOOKUP(lookup value,range,row index,lookup)

The HLOOKUP function has these four arguments:

■ **lookup value**

This is the value which you want to look for

■ **range**

This is the horizontal group of cells where you want to look for the value, and should include at least 2 part rows, the row containing the value, and the row holding the values to return, usually referred to as a table of values.

■ **row index**

This is the value counting rows from the search row as 1, to the row holding the values to return, or the row number within the table.

■ **lookup**

This is either TRUE or FALSE, and specifies whether or not you want the function to find an exact match to the lookup value, or an approximate match. If TRUE or omitted, an approximate match is returned if an exact match is not found; this requires the lookup cells to be sorted in ascending order.

Look at the example on the next page and read the explanatory text that follows.

We have entered data in rows 6,7,8 giving the diameter, length and price of a selection of tools.

In cell B4 we have entered a diameter and we want to look up the length and price for this diameter.

In cell C4 where we want to display the length for a specific diameter, we have created the HLOOKUP formula as follows:

=HLOOKUP(B4, B6:H8,2,FALSE)

Cell B4 is the value we want to find.

Cells B6:H8 contain all the information we are wanting to look up; this is effectively a table.

The row containing the value we want to return is effectively the 2nd row (Length) in the block of cells containing the data.

We want to return only an exact match for the diameter we specify, so the final parameter is FALSE.

Similarly if we now want to look up the price, see the image below

In cell D4 where we want to display the price for a specific diameter, we have created the HLOOKUP formula as follows:

=HLOOKUP(B4, B6:H8,3,FALSE)

Here B4 is again the value we want to find.

Cells B6:H8 contain all the information we are wanting to look up; they are effectively a table.

This time, the row containing the value we want to return is the 3nd row (price) in the block of cells containing the data.

We want to return only an exact match for the diameter we specify, so the final parameter is FALSE.

Having put all this together, if we look at the image below, we can see that the lookups pull through the values from the table as required.

	A	B	C	D	E	F	G	H
1	Tool sizes							
2								
3		Diameter	Length	Price				
4	Search for	1.5	4	£2.00				
5								
6	Diameter	0.5	1	1.5	2	2.5	3	3.5
7	Length	3	3	4	4	5	5	6
8	Price	£1.50	£1.75	£2.00	£2.00	£2.25	£2.50	£2.60
9								
10								

D6 — fx 1.5

Sheet1 / Sheet2 / Sheet3

We see Length 4, and Price £2.00 in cells C4 and D4 respectively, which have been correctly pulled from the table of data.

VLOOKUP

The V in VLOOKUP is to identify that the function searches in a vertical direction, ie down columns.

The function searches for a value in a particular column. If the value is found, it returns the matching value in the same row, from a specified column to the right of the column being searched.

=VLOOKUP(lookup value,range,col index,lookup)

The VLOOKUP function syntax has these arguments:

■ **lookup value**

This is the value which you want to look for

■ **range**

This is the horizontal group of cells where you want to look for the value, and should include at least 2 part columns, the column containing the value, and the column holding the values to return, usually referred to as a table of values.

■ **col index**

This is the value counting columns from the search column as 1, to the column holding the values to return, or the column number within the table.

■ **lookup**

This optional argument is either TRUE or FALSE, and specifies whether or not you want the function to find an exact match to the lookup value, or an approximate match. If TRUE or omitted, an approximate match is returned if an exact match is not found; this requires the lookup cells to be sorted in ascending order.

Look at the example below and read the explanatory text that follows.

	COUNT	▼	✕ ✓ *fx*	=VLOOKUP(B3,A6:B17,2,FALSE)		⊻
	A	B		VLOOKUP(lookup_value, table_array, col_index_num, [		
1	Products					
2						
3	Lookup inventory code	p133		Quantity	2,FALSE)	
4						
5	Inventory Code	Quantity				
6	A1	12				
7	A3	34				
8	B4	22				
9	A5	1				
10	D6	89				
11	H8	900				
12	K5	31				
13	S9	451				
14	C3	67				
15	P133	76				
16	A112	32				
17	W34	90				
18						

Sheet1　Sheet2　Sheet3

We have entered data in columns A and B giving the inventory (stock) code, and quantity for a group of products.

In cell B3 we have entered an inventory code and we want to look up the quantity held for this Inventory Code.

In cell E3 where we want to display the quantity for this inventory code, we have created the VLOOKUP formula as follows:

=VLOOKUP(B3, A6:B17,2,FALSE)

Here B3 is the value we want to find.

Cells A6:B17 contain all the information we are wanting to look up, effectively a table (only 2 columns).

The column we want to return is effectively the 2nd column (Quantity) in the block of cells containing the data.

We want to return only an exact match for the inventory code we specify, so the final parameter is FALSE.

If you look at the image below, you can see that the formula returns 76, the quantity for inventory code P133.

	E3	▼	*fx*	=VLOOKUP(B3,A6:B17,2,FALSE)		
	A	B	C	D	E	F
1	Products					
2						
3	Lookup inventory code	p133		Quantity	76	
4						
5	Inventory Code	Quantity				
6	A1	12				
7	A3	34				
8	B4	22				
9	A5	1				
10	D6	89				
11	H8	900				
12	K5	31				
13	S9	451				
14	C3	67				
15	P133	76				
16	A112	32				
17	W34	90				
18						

Sheet1 / Sheet2 / Sheet3

notes on lookups

■ When doing a lookup for a text value, the search does not distinguish between upper and lower case text, they are both regarded as the same.

■ If you want to return an approximate value if an exact match cannot be found, the search data must be in ascending order.

circular references

A **Circular Reference** occurs when a cell containing a formula includes its own cell reference in the formula. A simple example would be if cell B8 held the formula =sum(B2:B8)

When this occurs you will be given a warning, as shown in the image below.

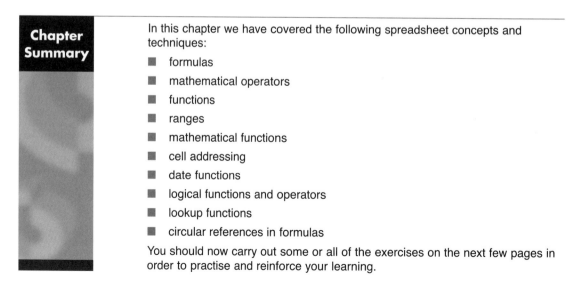

To remove the error, select OK and correct the formula in the cell.

Chapter Summary	In this chapter we have covered the following spreadsheet concepts and techniques:

■ formulas

■ mathematical operators

■ functions

■ ranges

■ mathematical functions

■ cell addressing

■ date functions

■ logical functions and operators

■ lookup functions

■ circular references in formulas

You should now carry out some or all of the exercises on the next few pages in order to practise and reinforce your learning.

Activities

Exercise 1 – using formulas and modifying formats

In this first exercise we will open an existing spreadsheet containing some data, introduce some formulas, use the basic operators (+, -, /, *), and making use of ranges and absolute cell references.

To access this spreadsheet visit www.osbornebooks.co.uk ('Resources'), and download **T4investment**

Stage 1

This stage is about starting to introduce some formulas into our spreadsheet, and using the basic arithmetic operators (+, -, /, *).

1. Download the workbook **T4investment**

2. Open the downloaded file, save the workbook with new name **T4Exercise1**

   The workbook should appear as shown below.

	A	B	C	D	E	F	
1	Investment Portfolio						
2							
3					Annual	Weekly	
4		Year start	Year end		Interest	interest	
5	Where	Amount	Amount	Interest	Rate	Amount	
6		£	£	£	%	£	
7	Bank1	£500	£512.50				
8	Bank2	£4,000	£4,100.33				
9	Building Society1	£2,000	£2,100.00				
10	Building Society2	£3,000	£3,099.99				
11	Post Office	£100	£102.95				
12	Bonds1	£1,000	£1,201.54				
13	Bonds2	£2,000	£2,095.00				

3. The first formula we want to enter is to calculate the interest which has been added to each investment. Enter formulas in column D to calculate the interest. (Taking the Year start amount from the Year end amount).

4. Format the interest column (D) to display with the pound symbol (£)

5. We want to calculate the interest rate for each investment. Enter formulas in column E for the interest rate as a decimal. (Take the interest divided by the Year start amount)

6. Display Annual Interest Rate as a percentage with 2 decimal places.

7. We now want to calculate how much interest we were getting weekly. Enter formulas in column F to calculate the weekly amount of interest. (Use the interest column D, and divide it by 52).

8. Format the weekly interest column to display with the pound symbol, and 2 decimal places.

9. Save the workbook with the same name **T4Exercise1**

Your spreadsheet should appear as follows:

	A	B	C	D	E	F
1	Investment Portfolio					
2						
3					Annual	Weekly
4		Year start	Year end		Interest	interest
5	Where	Amount	Amount	Interest	Rate	Amount
6		£	£	£	%	£
7	Bank1	£500	£512.50	£12.50	2.50%	£0.24
8	Bank2	£4,000	£4,100.33	£100.33	2.51%	£1.93
9	Building Society1	£2,000	£2,100.00	£100.00	5.00%	£1.92
10	Building Society2	£3,000	£3,099.99	£99.99	3.33%	£1.92
11	Post Office	£100	£102.95	£2.95	2.95%	£0.06
12	Bonds1	£1,000	£1,201.54	£201.54	20.15%	£3.88
13	Bonds2	£2,000	£2,095.00	£95.00	4.75%	£1.83

The image below also shows the formulas used to perform the calculations.

	A	B	C	D	E	F
1	Investment Portfolio					
2						
3					Annual	Weekly
4		Year start	Year end		Interest	interest
5	Where	Amount	Amount	Interest	Rate	Amount
6		£	£	£	%	£
7	Bank1	500	512.5	=C7-B7	=D7/B7	=D7/52
8	Bank2	4000	4100.33	=C8-B8	=D8/B8	=D8/52
9	Building Society1	2000	2100	=C9-B9	=D9/B9	=D9/52
10	Building Society2	3000	3099.99	=C10-B10	=D10/B10	=D10/52
11	Post Office	100	102.95	=C11-B11	=D11/B11	=D11/52
12	Bonds1	1000	1201.54	=C12-B12	=D12/B12	=D12/52
13	Bonds2	2000	2095	=C13-B13	=D13/B13	=D13/52

Stage 2

In this stage, we are going to continue to extend the calculations using autosum, and modify the formatting.

1. We want to introduce some totals in row 14. In cell A14, enter **Totals**

2. Using **AUTOSUM** (if available, if not, just manually use **SUM( )**). Enter a formula in cell B14 to total the year start amounts.

3. Similarly, again using **AUTOSUM**, total the year end amounts, into cell C14.

4. Format cells B14 and C14 with a border along the bottom of the cells, style thin double line.

5. In cell D16 enter the text **Received**.

6. In cells A17,B17,C17,D17 respectively, enter:

Special bonds	£1,000	£1,000	£100.00

7. Enter a formula in cell E17 to calculate the Annual Interest Rate.

8. In cell F17, enter a formula to calculate the Weekly Interest Amount.

9. Delete row 2 to close the gap at the top.

10. Save your spreadsheet (keeping the same name – **T4Exercise1**)

    Your spreadsheet should now appear as shown below:

	A	B	C	D	E	F	G
1	Investment Portfolio						
2					Annual	Weekly	
3		Year start	Year end		Interest	interest	
4	Where	Amount	Amount	Interest	Rate	Amount	
5		£	£	£	%	£	
6	Bank1	£500	£512.50	£12.50	2.50%	£0.24	
7	Bank2	£4,000	£4,100.33	£100.33	2.51%	£1.93	
8	Building Society1	£2,000	£2,100.00	£100.00	5.00%	£1.92	
9	Building Society2	£3,000	£3,099.99	£99.99	3.33%	£1.92	
10	Post Office	£100	£102.95	£2.95	2.95%	£0.06	
11	Bonds1	£1,000	£1,201.54	£201.54	20.15%	£3.88	
12	Bonds2	£2,000	£2,095.00	£95.00	4.75%	£1.83	
13	Totals	£12,600	£13,212.31				
14							
15				Received			
16	Special bonds	£1,000	£1,000.00	£100.00	10.00%	£1.92	

Stage 3

We are now going to use ranges, conditional formatting and absolute addressing.

1.   Move the Totals row (row13) to the row below Special bonds (row 17)

2.   Delete rows 13,14,15 to move Special bonds to be directly next to Bonds (row 12)

3.   On the totals row, cell B14, manually edit the range in the formula to include cell B13.

4.   Similarly for cell C14, edit the range in the formula to include cell C13.

5   Apply conditional formatting to display the interest rate in a bold and italic typeface for all entries where the interest rate is greater than 3%.

6.   In cell G3, enter **Maximum**

7.   In cell G4, enter **Interest**

8.   In cell G5 enter £, aligned in the centre.

9.   Create a formula to calculate the maximum interest which would have been earned, if each investment had received the largest interest rate (cell E11) in cell G6, ie year start amount multiplied by this interest rate. Use absolute addressing for cell E11 within the formula.

10.   Copy the formula to G7 through to G13

11   Add a final column in column H, in cell H3 enter **Lost**, in H4, enter **Interest**, in cell H5 enter £, aligned in the centre.

12.   In cell H13 enter a formula to calculate the difference between the Maximum Interest (column G) and the Interest (column D).

13.   Copy the formula from cell H13 to cells H12 through to H6.

14.   Change the font colour to red for cells H6 through to H13.

15.   Save your spreadsheet (keeping the same name - **T4Exercise1**)

Your spreadsheet should now look as shown below. Note that the red text shows here as grey.

	A	B	C	D	E	F	G	H
1	Investment Portfolio							
2					Annual	Weekly		
3		Year start	Year end		Interest	interest	Maximum	Lost
4	Where	Amount	Amount	Interest	Rate	Amount	Interest	Interest
5		£	£	£	%	£	£	£
6	Bank1	£500	£512.50	£12.50	2.50%	£0.24	£100.77	£88.27
7	Bank2	£4,000	£4,100.33	£100.33	2.51%	£1.93	£806.16	£705.83
8	Building Society1	£2,000	£2,100.00	£100.00	5.00%	£1.92	£403.08	£303.08
9	Building Society2	£3,000	£3,099.99	£99.99	3.33%	£1.92	£604.62	£504.63
10	Post Office	£100	£102.95	£2.95	2.95%	£0.06	£20.15	£17.20
11	Bonds1	£1,000	£1,201.54	£201.54	20.15%	£3.88	£201.54	£0.00
12	Bonds2	£2,000	£2,095.00	£95.00	4.75%	£1.83	£403.08	£308.08
13	Special bonds	£1,000	£1,000.00	£100.00	10.00%	£1.92	£201.54	£101.54
14	Totals	£13,600	£14,212.31					

The image below also shows the formulas used to perform the calculations

	A	B	C	D	E	F	G	H
1	Investment Portfo							
2					Annual	Weekly		
3		Year start	Year end		Interest	interest	Maximum	Lost
4	Where	Amount	Amount	Interest	Rate	Amount	Interest	Interest
5		£	£	£	%	£	£	£
6	Bank1	500	512.5	=C6-B6	=D6/B6	=D6/52	=B6*$E$11	=G6-D6
7	Bank2	4000	4100.33	=C7-B7	=D7/B7	=D7/52	=B7*$E$11	=G7-D7
8	Building Society1	2000	2100	=C8-B8	=D8/B8	=D8/52	=B8*$E$11	=G8-D8
9	Building Society2	3000	3099.99	=C9-B9	=D9/B9	=D9/52	=B9*$E$11	=G9-D9
10	Post Office	100	102.95	=C10-B10	=D10/B10	=D10/52	=B10*$E$11	=G10-D10
11	Bonds1	1000	1201.54	=C11-B11	=D11/B11	=D11/52	=B11*$E$11	=G11-D11
12	Bonds2	2000	2095	=C12-B12	=D12/B12	=D12/52	=B12*$E$11	=G12-D12
13	Special bonds	1000	1000	100	=D13/B13	=D13/52	=B13*$E$11	=G13-D13
14	Totals	=SUM(B6:B13)	=SUM(C6:C13)					
15								

You have now completed the first exercise.

Exercise 2 – using numerical and date functions, and conditional logic

In this next exercise we are going to use more of the numerical and date functions, together with some conditional logic (IF statements). We are again going to make use of an existing spreadsheet.

Visit the website www.osbornebooks.co.uk ('Resources') to download the spreadsheet **T4employee**

Stage 1

This stage is utilising built in functions within a previously created workbook.

1.   Download the workbook **T4employee**

2.   Open the downloaded file, save the workbook with new name **T4Exercise2**

3.   The workbook should appear as shown below.

	A	B	C	D	E	F	G
1	Employee records						
2							
3						Calculated	Age
4	Surname	Birth Date	Start Date	Department	Salary	Age	Years
5	Johal	02/03/1975	01/06/2000	Sales	20000		
6	Jones	14/10/1963	01/07/2001	HR	16000		
7	Wakula	03/09/1978	01/07/2002	Sales	20000		
8	White	30/06/1967	03/01/2009	Accounts	15000		
9	Hacek	24/05/1970	01/07/2010	Accounts	18000		
10	Bhopal	12/02/1978	01/07/2010	Sales	20500		
11	Plant	19/03/1976	01/09/2010	Sales	21500		
12							

4.   In cell D1, enter **Date**

5.   In cell E1, enter a formula to display today's date, in the format dd/mm/yyyy.

6.   In cell F5, we want to create a formula to display the person's age. To do this we will need to use today's date (cell E1), the birth date (cell B5), and convert the difference between the two into years, by dividing by 365. (Note: you will need to use brackets to obtain the correct result.)

7.   Once you have created the formula and visually checked that it gives the correct result, edit the formula to make the reference to cell E1 (today's date) an absolute address.

8.   Copy the formula to cells F6 through to F11.

9.   In column G, create a formula, which gives the calculated age (Column F) as a whole number of years only, using the INT function, apply the formula to cells G5 through to G11.

10.   Format the column G to display with no decimal places.

11.   Save your spreadsheet (keeping the same name – **T4Exercise2**).

Your spreadsheet should now look as shown below:-

	A	B	C	D	E	F	G
1	Employee records			Date	11/11/2010		
2							
3						Calculated	Age
4	Surname	Birth Date	Start Date	Department	Salary	Age	Years
5	Johal	02/03/1975	01/06/2000	Sales	20000	35.72	35
6	Jones	14/10/1963	01/07/2001	HR	16000	47.11	47
7	Wakula	03/09/1978	01/07/2002	Sales	20000	32.21	32
8	White	30/06/1967	03/01/2009	Accounts	15000	43.40	43
9	Hacek	24/05/1970	01/07/2010	Accounts	18000	40.50	40
10	Bhopal	12/02/1978	01/07/2010	Sales	20500	32.77	32
11	Plant	19/03/1976	01/09/2010	Sales	21500	34.67	34
12							

The image below displays the formulas used to perform the calculations.

	A	B	C	D	E	F	G
1	Employee			Date	=TODAY()		
2							
3						Calculated	Age
4	Surname	Birth Date	Start Date	Department	Salary	Age	Years
5	Johal	27455	36678	Sales	20000	=($E$1-B5)/365	=INT(F5)
6	Jones	23298	37073	HR	16000	=($E$1-B6)/365	=INT(F6)
7	Wakula	28736	37438	Sales	20000	=($E$1-B7)/365	=INT(F7)
8	White	24653	39816	Accounts	15000	=($E$1-B8)/365	=INT(F8)
9	Hacek	25712	40360	Accounts	18000	=($E$1-B9)/365	=INT(F9)
10	Bhopal	28533	40360	Sales	20500	=($E$1-B10)/365	=INT(F10)
11	Plant	27838	40422	Sales	21500	=($E$1-B11)/365	=INT(F11)
12							

Stage 2

We are going to make some changes to the format, and enter some more formulas.

1. Format the salary data (column E), so that each value displays with the 1000 separator (,) and no decimal places.

2. Hide columns F and G.

3. Make all text in rows 3 and 4 (our column headings) bold and underlined.

4. Enter **Service**, in cell H3, **Award** in cell H4 (make sure they are bold and underlined)

5. Insert a row between rows 2 and 3

6. In cell A3, enter *Award date* in italics, widen column A so that this text fits within the column.

7. In cell B3, enter 01/01/2005. Ensure it is formatted as a date.

8. We are going to use a formula in column H to calculate whether or not an employee was employed before 1st January 2005, and may receive a service award. You are to use the IF( ) function to do the calculation, and cell B3 (where the date to compare against has been entered).

   For example to calculate H6, IF the value in C6 is before (less than) B3 THEN "yes", OTHERWISE "no").

9. Modify the formula to use the absolute address of cell B3.

10. Once you are happy with the formula in cell H6, copy the formula to cells H7 through to H12.

11. Save the workbook with the name **T4Exercise2**

    Your spreadsheet should appear as follows:

	A	B	C	D	E	H
1	Employee records			Date	11/11/2010	
2						
3	*Award date*	01/01/2005				
4						Service
5	Surname	Birth Date	Start Date	Department	Salary	Award
6	Johal	02/03/1975	01/06/2000	Sales	20,000	yes
7	Jones	14/10/1963	01/07/2001	HR	16,000	yes
8	Wakula	03/09/1978	01/07/2002	Sales	20,000	yes
9	White	30/06/1967	03/01/2009	Accounts	15,000	no
10	Hacek	24/05/1970	01/07/2010	Accounts	18,000	no
11	Bhopal	12/02/1978	01/07/2010	Sales	20,500	no
12	Plant	19/03/1976	01/09/2010	Sales	21,500	no

The image on the next page displays the formulas used to perform the calculations.

	A	B	C	D	E	H
1	Employee re			Date	=TODAY()	
2						
3	*Award date*	38353				
4						Service
5	**Surname**	**Birth Date**	**Start Date**	**Department**	**Salary**	**Award**
6	Johal	27455	36678	Sales	20000	=IF(C6<$B$3,"yes","no")
7	Jones	23298	37073	HR	16000	=IF(C7<$B$3,"yes","no")
8	Wakula	28736	37438	Sales	20000	=IF(C8<$B$3,"yes","no")
9	White	24653	39816	Accounts	15000	=IF(C9<$B$3,"yes","no")
10	Hacek	25712	40360	Accounts	18000	=IF(C10<$B$3,"yes","no")
11	Bhopal	28533 24/05/1970		Sales	20500	=IF(C11<$B$3,"yes","no")
12	Plant	27838	40422	Sales	21500	=IF(C12<$B$3,"yes","no")
13						

Stage 3

We are now going to do some more calculations.

1. Enter **New**, in cell I4, **Salary** in cell I5 (make sure they are bold and underlined)

2. We are going to calculate new salaries, to populate column I. All those in the Sales Department are getting a pay rise of £200, all other departments are only going to receive £100. You are to use the IF( ) function to do the calculation.

    For example to calculate I6, IF the value in D6 is "Sales" THEN E6 add £200, OTHERWISE E6 add £100).

3. Once you are happy with the formula in cell I6, copy the formula to cells I7 through to I12.

4. Format the new salary data (column I), so that each value displays with the 1000 separator (,) and no decimal places.

5. Save the workbook with the name **T4Exercise2**

Your spreadsheet should appear as follows:

	A	B	C	D	E	H	I
1	Employee records			Date	11/11/2010		
2							
3	*Award date*	01/01/2005					
4						Service	New
5	**Surname**	**Birth Date**	**Start Date**	**Department**	**Salary**	**Award**	**Salary**
6	Johal	02/03/1975	01/06/2000	Sales	20,000	yes	20,200
7	Jones	14/10/1963	01/07/2001	HR	16,000	yes	16,100
8	Wakula	03/09/1978	01/07/2002	Sales	20,000	yes	20,200
9	White	30/06/1967	03/01/2009	Accounts	15,000	no	15,100
10	Hacek	24/05/1970	01/07/2010	Accounts	18,000	no	18,100
11	Bhopal	12/02/1978	01/07/2010	Sales	20,500	no	20,700
12	Plant	19/03/1976	01/09/2010	Sales	21,500	no	21,700

The image below also shows the formulas behind the calculations

	A	B	C	D	E	H	I
1	Employee re			Date	=TODAY()		
2							
3	Award date	38353					
4						Service	New
5	Surname	Birth Date	Start Date	Department	Salary	Award	Salary
6	Johal	27455	36678	Sales	20000	=IF(C6<$B$3,"yes","no")	=IF(D6="sales",E6+200,E6+100)
7	Jones	23298	37073	HR	16000	=IF(C7<$B$3,"yes","no")	=IF(D7="sales",E7+200,E7+100)
8	Wakula	28736	37438	Sales	20000	=IF(C8<$B$3,"yes","no")	=IF(D8="sales",E8+200,E8+100)
9	White	24653	39816	Accounts	15000	=IF(C9<$B$3,"yes","no")	=IF(D9="sales",E9+200,E9+100)
10	Hacek	25712	40360	Accounts	18000	=IF(C10<$B$3,"yes","no")	=IF(D10="sales",E10+200,E10+100)
11	Bhopal	28533	40360	Sales	20500	=IF(C11<$B$3,"yes","no")	=IF(D11="sales",E11+200,E11+100)
12	Plant	27838	40422	Sales	21500	=IF(C12<$B$3,"yes","no")	=IF(D12="sales",E12+200,E12+100)

You have now completed the second exercise.

Exercise 3 – using VLOOKUP

In this next exercise we are going to use the VLOOKUP function. We are again going to make use of an existing spreadsheet.

To access this spreadsheet visit www.osbornebooks.co.uk ('Resources') to download the spreadsheet **T4inventory**.

Stage 1

This stage uses VLOOKUP with a previously created workbook.

Note: if you enter the formula and the cell displays #N/A this means that the value you are trying to find does not exist in the data range through which you are searching – check the formula thoroughly.

1. Download the workbook **T4inventory**

2. Open the downloaded file, save the workbook with new name **T4Exercise3**

    The workbook should appear as shown below.

	A	B	C	D
1	Warehouse information			
2				
3				
4	Code	Bin	Price	
5	ab1	1	£2.00	
6	ab2	2	£30.00	
7	ab3	1	£27.00	
8	ab4	1	£14.00	
9	ab5	3	£21.00	
10	ab6	4	£12.00	
11	ab7	1	£7.00	
12	ab8	2	£24.00	
13	ab9	1	£27.00	

Sheet1 / Sheet

3. Use the scroll bars to move up and down the data. You can see that it gets harder to pick out individual items once we start to work with more data. Return to the top of the data.

4. Insert a row between rows 2 and 3

5. In cell A3, enter **Product?**, cell C3 enter **Bin**, E3 enter **Price**

6. In Cell B3 enter **fr4**

7. In cell D3 enter the formula to lookup the Bin number from the data below, for the product code specified in cell B3.
    (Use VLOOKUP on cell B3, specifying the lookup range to include codes and bin data only).

8. In cell F3 enter the formula to lookup the price from the data below, for the product code in cell B3.

   (Use VLOOKUP on cell B3, specifying the lookup range to include codes, bin and price data only)

9. Format cell F3 to display **Currency (£ pounds)**.

10. Save the workbook with the name **T4Exercise3**.

    The workbook should appear as shown below.

	A	B	C	D	E	F
1	Warehouse information					
2						
3	Product?	fr4	Bin		4 Price	£7.00
4						
5	Code	Bin	Price			
6	ab1		1	£2.00		
7	ab2		2	£30.00		
8	ab3		1	£27.00		
9	ab4		1	£14.00		
10	ab5		3	£21.00		
11	ab6		4	£12.00		

The formulas are shown in the image below.

	A	B	C	D	E	F
1	Wareh					
2						
3	Product?	fr4	Bin	=VLOOKUP(B3,A6:B51,2,FALSE)	Price	=VLOOKUP(B3,A6:C51,3,FALSE)
4						
5	Code	Bin	Price			
6	ab1	1	2			
7	ab2	2	30			
8	ab3	1	27			
9	ab4	1	14			
10	ab5	3	21			

Stage 2

We will now make some small modifications to the spreadsheet.

1.   Insert 2 rows between row 4 and row 5.

2.   In cell A5, enter **Product2?**, cell C5 enter **Bin2**, E5 enter **Price2**

3.   In Cell B5 enter **ab1**

4.   In cell D5 enter the formula to lookup the Bin number from the data below, for the product code specified in cell B5.

      (Use VLOOKUP on cell B5, specifying the lookup range to include codes and bin data only).

5.   In cell F5 enter the formula to lookup the price from the data below, for the product code in cell B5.

      (Use VLOOKUP on cell B5, specifying the lookup range to include codes, bin and price data only).

6.   Format cell F5 to display **Currency (£ pounds)**.

7.   Modify the first product code to be looked up in B3, change this to be code dd4.

8.   Move to cell A1

9.   Save the workbook with the name **T4Exercise3**. The workbook should appear as shown below.

	A	B	C	D	E	F
1	Warehouse information					
2						
3	Product?	dd4	Bin	10	Price	£19.00
4						
5	Product2?	ab1	Bin2	1	Price2	£2.00
6						
7	**Code**	**Bin**	**Price**			
8	ab1		1	£2.00		
9	ab2		2	£30.00		
10	ab3		1	£27.00		
11	ab4		1	£14.00		
12	ab5		3	£21.00		

The formulas are shown in the image below.

	A	B	C	D	E	F
1	Warehor					
2						
3	Product?	dd4	Bin	=VLOOKUP(B3,A8:B53,2,FALSE)	Price	=VLOOKUP(B3,A8:C53,3,FALSE)
4						
5	Product2?	ab1	Bin2	=VLOOKUP(B5,A8:B53,2,FALSE)	Price2	=VLOOKUP(B5,A8:C53,3,FALSE)
6						

Exercise 4 – using HLOOKUP

In this next exercise we are going to use the HLOOKUP function. We are again going to make use of an existing spreadsheet.

To access this spreadsheet visit www.osbornebooks.co.uk ('Resources') to download the spreadsheet **T4inventoryhoriz**

Stage 1

This stage is using HLOOKUP with a previously created workbook.

Note: if you enter the formula and the cell displays #N/A this means that the value you are trying to find does not exist in the data range through which you are searching – check the formula thoroughly.

1.   Download the workbook **T4inventoryhoriz**

2.   Open the downloaded file, save the workbook with new name **T4Exercise4**

3.   The workbook should appear as shown below. This is the same data as before, but it has been entered horizontally.

	A	B	C	D	E	F	G	H	I	J	K
1	Warehouse information										
2											
3											
4	Code	ab1	ab2	ab3	ab4	ab5	ab6	ab7	ab8	ab9	ab10
5	Bin	1	2	1	1	3	4	1	2	1	5
6	Price	£2.00	£30.00	£27.00	£14.00	£21.00	£12.00	£7.00	£24.00	£27.00	£50.00
7											
8											
9											

4.   In cell A8, enter **Product?**, cell C8 enter **Price**, E8 enter **Bin**

5.   In Cell B8 enter **ad11**

6.   In cell D8 enter the formula to lookup the price from the data above, for the product code specified in cell B8.

   (Use HLOOKUP on cell B8, specifying the lookup range to include codes, bin and price data).

7.   Format cell D8 to display **Currency (£ pounds)**.

8.   In cell F8 enter the formula to lookup the bin from the data above, for the product code in cell B8.

   (Use HLOOKUP on cell B8, specifying the lookup range to include codes, bin and price data).

9.   Save the workbook with the name **T4Exercise4**. The workbook should appear as shown in the image on the next page.

	A	B	C	D	E	F	G	H	I	J	K
1	Warehouse information										
2											
3											
4	Code	ab1	ab2	ab3	ab4	ab5	ab6	ab7	ab8	ab9	ab10
5	Bin	1	2	1	1	3	4	1	2	1	5
6	Price		£2.00	£30.00	£27.00	£14.00	£21.00	£12.00	£7.00	£24.00	£27.00	£50.00
7											
8	Product?	ad11	Price	£18.00	Bin		12				
9											

The formulas are shown in the image below.

	A	B	C	D	E	F
1	Wareh					
2						
3						
4	Code	ab1	ab2	ab3		ab4	ab5
5	Bin	1	2	1		1	3
6	Price	2	30	27		14	21
7						
8	Product?	ad11	Price	=HLOOKUP(B8,B4:AU6,3,FALSE)	Bin	=HLOOKUP(B8,B4:AU6,2,FALSE)
9						

5 Sorting, checking and importing data

this chapter covers...

This chapter covers the tools which are regularly available within spreadsheet packages, and shows how you can move data between spreadsheets and other documents. It explains and takes you through the concepts and techniques listed below. By the time you have finished this chapter and carried out the exercises which follow, you should be able to organise your spreadsheet to include subtotals, and be able to transfer information between spreadsheets and other software packages.

The concepts and techniques covered are:

■ formula validation

■ spell check

■ find and replace

■ sorting and filtering data

■ introducing subtotals

■ linking and embedding data

■ importing and exporting data

Note that the the step-by-step instructions given in this chapter are based on the Microsoft® Excel model, but the concepts and techniques described relate to all spreadsheet packages.

FORMULA VALIDATION

We have explained formulas and how to create them earlier in this book. We are now going to explain some of the ways of checking that the formulas we have entered are doing what we expect them to do. The methods which we are going to cover are:

- show formulas

- error checking

- trace precedents

- trace dependents

show formulas

This is a simple visual method, where formulas are displayed within the sheet. The example below shows the worksheet displayed in the normal way:

	A	B	C	D	E	F	G
	A13			f_x			
1	Bank transactions						
2							
3	Opening balance	1,500.00					
4	Closing balance	1,289.05			**Down		
5							
6	Date	Debit	Credit	Balance			
7	02/07/2010	95.34	0.00	1,404.66			
8	11/07/2010	0.00	25.50	1,430.16			
9	15/07/2010	0.00	34.78	1,464.94			
10	22/07/2010	67.90	0.00	1,397.04			
11	28/07/2010	107.99	0.00	1,289.05			
12	Totals	271.23	60.28		1,289.05		

We then select **Show Formulas** (or its equivalent within your package) and the way in which the cells display changes as shown below:

	A	B	C	D	E
	A1		f_x	Bank transactions	
1	Bank transactions				
2					
3	Opening balance	1500			
4	Closing balance	=D11			=IF(B4<B3,"**Down","")
5					
6	Date	Debit	Credit	Balance	
7	40361	95.34	0	=B3-B7+C7	
8	40370	0	25.5	=D7-B8+C8	
9	40374	0	34.78	=D8-B9+C9	
10	40381	67.9	0	=D9-B10+C10	
11	40387	107.99	0	=D10-B11+C11	
12	Totals	=SUM(B7:B11)	=SUM(C7:C11)		=B3-B12+C12

In the screen at the bottom of the previous page are displayed the actual data or formulas contained in each cell.

In column A where we have dates, for example, what we now see is the serial number representation of the date (as described on page 82). Similarly column D shows the mathematical formulas used to calculate the running balance of the bank account.

In a relatively small worksheet, or a particular section of a larger worksheet, it is easy to check that the formulas that have been entered are correct by using the **Show Formulas** option.

It is possible to print the worksheet in this form using the normal print options.

To revert to the normal display we select **Show Formulas** again from the menu bar and select the appropriate command.

As mentioned, this is a fairly basic way of checking formulas. There is a more automated way using a facility called **error checking**, which is available in most spreadsheet packages.

error checking

The **error checking** facility checks for common errors which occur in formulas. These include:

■   formulas that result in an error, such as dividing by zero

■   numbers formatted as text, or preceded by an apostrophe (')

■   formulas inconsistent with other formulas near them

■   formulas which omit cells which are near others which have been included in the formula (eg a range of cells)

■   cells containing circular references

Any cells where the formula is in error are flagged with a small green triangle in the upper-left corner of the cell.

In the same way that we can have our word processing package checking for errors as we type, it is possible to set the spreadsheet package options, so that our formulas are checked as we enter them; this is known as **automatic error checking**. Alternatively we can use the **error checking facility** at any time to check through the whole worksheet.

If we take the Bank transactions spreadsheet shown on the previous page we can modify the formula in cell D9:

from	**=D8-B9+C9**
to	**=D8-B10+C9**

You can see in the image below, that when we have automatic checking on, we get a small triangle in the upper left of the cell D9, indicating a formula error.

	A	B	C	D	E
1	Bank transactions				
2					
3	Opening balance	1,500.00			
4	Closing balance	1,221.15			**Down
5					
6	Date	Debit	Credit	Balance	
7	02/07/2010	95.34	0.00	1,404.66	
8	11/07/2010	0.00	25.50	1,430.16	
9	15/07/2010	0.00	34.78	1,397.04	

If we then select cell D9 we get an exclamation icon and a description of the error – 'Inconsistent Formula' – which tells us that this formula does not match the pattern of the formulas above and below (or to either side in the same row.) Here cell D9 is inconsistent with the formulas in Column D.

	Debit	Credit	Balance		
010	95.34	0.00	1,404.66		
010	0.00	25.50	1,430.16		
010	0.00	⚠ ▾	1,397.04		
010	67.90		Inconsistent Formula		
010	107.99		Copy Formula from Above		
	271.23		Help on this error		
			Ignore Error		
			Edit in Formula Bar		
July	Sheet3		Error Checking Options...		

To set your choices for error checking:

■ Select **Options** from the appropriate menu

■ Select **Formulas**

■ Either check or uncheck **Background error checking** as required

■ Check or uncheck the **Rules** to configure as you require

Note that if the formula is actually what we want we can instruct the error check to **ignore the erro**r.

To perform a full worksheet error check:

■ Select **Error check** (or its equivalent) from the menu

The rules will be applied as set up in the Options described on the previous page, and any cells with a formula error will be flagged as shown on the previous page.

circular references

As mentioned previously, this occurs when a cell's formula contains a reference to itself. The **Error Checking** menu displays a drop down list and one of the items in the list is **Circular References**. Clicking this item will cause a list of those cells containing circular references to be displayed. If you click on any of the cells in the list, the cursor will move to that cell and you can edit the formula. When all circular references have been resolved, the list will be empty.

trace precedents

The **Trace Precedents** facility allows you to identify those cells which affect the value of the currently selected cell.

For example if cell D4 contained the formula

   =A3 +B3

Both A3 and B3 would be **precedents** of D4, since they both affect the value of D4.

If we take the Bank transactions worksheet illustrated on the last few pages as an example, if we select cell E12, which holds the formula

   =B3-B12+C12

and then select **Trace Precedents** from the formulas menu, we can see the result as shown below.

	E12	▼		f_x	=B3-B12+C12		≫
	A	B	C	D	E	F	
1	Bank transactions						
2							
3	Opening balance	1,500.00					
4	Closing balance	1,289.05			**Down		
5							
6	Date	Debit	Credit	Balance			
7	02/07/2010	95.34	0.00	1,404.66			
8	11/07/2010	0.00	25.50	1,430.16			
9	15/07/2010	0.00	34.78	1,464.94			
10	22/07/2010	67.90	0.00	1,397.04			
11	28/07/2010	107.99	0.00	1,289.05			
12	Totals	271.23	60.28		1,289.05		

From this image you can see that the arrows indicate that cells B3, B12 and C12 all affect (ie are precedents of) the value E12.

If we were to select **Trace Precedents** for a second time without moving from the selected cell, we would see the cells which are precedents for B3, B12 and C12 are added to the picture, as shown below.

	A	B	C	D	E	F
	E12 ▼		f_x =B3-B12+C12			
1	Bank transactions					
2						
3	Opening balance	1,500.00				
4	Closing balance	1,289.05			**Down	
5						
6	Date	Debit	Credit	Balance		
7	02/07/2010	95.34	0.00	1,404.66		
8	11/07/2010	0.00	25.50	1,430.16		
9	15/07/2010	0.00	34.78	1,464.94		
10	22/07/2010	67.90	0.00	1,397.04		
11	28/07/2010	107.99	0.00	1,289.05		
12	Totals	271.23	60.28		1,289.05	

The arrows show that B12 utilises the cells B7 through to B11, and similarly C12 utilises the cells C7 through to C11.

This **Trace Precedents** tool is very useful for checking formulas, especially on more complex sheets.

To Trace Precedents for a particular cell:

■ Select the required cell

■ Select **Trace Precedents** from the menu bar (usually in the formulas section)

■ Repeat as required

To remove the arrows generated:

■ Select **Remove Arrows** from the menu bar

trace dependents

The **Trace Dependents** facility allows you to identify those cells which are affected by the value of the currently selected cell.

For example if cell D4 contained the formula

=22+F4/20

D4 would be a **dependent** of F4, because its value is dependent on the value of F4.

If we return to the Bank transactions worksheet again and select cell B3, the Opening balance value, and then select **Trace Dependents**, the screen will appear as follows:

From this image you can see that the arrows indicate that cell B3 is used in formulas in cells E4, D7 and E12, showing that cells E4, D7, E12 are all **dependent** on B3.

If we were to select **Trace Dependents** for a second time without moving from the selected cell, we would then see any cells affected by E4, D7 and E12 added to the picture, as shown below:

On this screen only cell D8 is affected by these cells, since it is dependent on D7, so we see one additional small arrow, showing this dependency.

To Trace Dependents for a particular cell:

- Select the required cell

- Select **Trace Dependents** from the menu bar (usually in the formulas section)

- Repeat as required

To remove the arrows generated:

- Select **Remove Arrows** from the menu bar

SPELL CHECK

Spreadsheet packages usually provide built-in **Spell checking** tools to check the text in your worksheets.

You can choose rules which you want to apply when performing a spell check – for example, to ignore words that are all uppercase.

To set your rule choices for Spell check:

- Select **Options** from the appropriate menu

- Select **Proofing**

- Check or uncheck the rules to configure as you require

You can request **Spell check** on just one cell or a **group of cells**.

To perform Spell check on a cell or group of cells:

- Select the required cell(s)

- Select **Spell check** (or its equivalent) from the menu

The rules will be applied as set up in the Options/Proofing described above, and any cells with a spelling error will be highlighted and suggestions for revised spellings offered.

To perform a full worksheet Spell check:

- Select **Spell check** (or its equivalent) from the menu

- Confirm that you wish to check the whole sheet

FIND AND REPLACE

find

Another powerful facility is the **Find** tool which can be used to find a specific value or text within the worksheet.

To use **Find**, select the **Find and Select** icon, select **Find** from the menu. As shown in the screen below, you then specify:-

Find what – this will be the value or text which is to be found (known as the **search string**):

If you chose **Find All**, all occurrences will be displayed together with their cell references allowing you to move to any one of them.

Find Next will find the first occurrence of the search string. You then click **Find Next** again to find the next one, and so on until there are no more to be found.

replace

The **Replace** tool enables you to find and replace specific text or values. To use this tool, select **Replace** from the **Find and Select** menu.

As you can see in the image below, you specify the value or text you want to find, and then the value or text which you want to replace it with (known as the **replacement string**):

If you chose **Replace All**, all occurrences of the **search string** will automatically be replaced with the **replacement string**.

Sometimes, you may only want to replace certain occurrences of the search string, in which case, you would select **Find Next**, until you find one which you want to change, and then you select **Replace** and then **Find Next** again until you have made all the changes you require.

Looking at the Work bookings example sheet below.

	A	B	C	D	E	F	
	A1			f_x	Work bookings		
1	Work bookings						
2							
3	Hourly rate	£20					
4							
5	**Client**	**Week1**	**Week2**	**Week3**	**Week4**	**Total**	
6	Smiths Ltd	15	15	15	15	60	
7	Jones and Partner	12	8	10	9	39	
8	Redwoods	13	20	11	7	51	

We could use **Find and Replace** to change the column titles from Week1, Week2 etc to be Month1, Month2 and so on. To do this:

- Select **Find and Replace** from the menu
- Find what – enter **Week**
- Replace with – enter **Month**
- Click **Replace All**

This is shown in the image below.

	A	B	C	D	E	F	G
	C1			f_x			
1	Work bookings						
2							
3	Hourly rate	£20					
4							
5	**Client**	**Week1**	**Week2**	**Week3**	**Week4**	**Total**	
6	Smi						
7	Jon						
8	Red						
9	Und						
10							
11							
12							
13							
14							

Find and Replace [?][X]

Find | Replace

Find what: Week

Replace with: Month

Options >>

Replace All | Replace | Find All | Find Next | Close

You can see the results in the screen below.

	A1	▼	⊙	f_x	Work bookings		⊗

	A	B	C	D	E	F	G
1	Work bookings						
2							
3	Hourly rate	£20					
4							
5	Client	Month1	Month2	Month3	Month4	Total	
6	Smiths Ltd	15	15	15	15	60	
7	Jones and Partner	12	8	10	9	39	
8	Redwoods	13	20	11	7	51	
9	Underhills	13	20	11	2	46	
10							

SORTING DATA – THE SORT TOOL

If we look at the worksheet (work bookings) shown in the image above, we can see that the client names are not in alphabetical order. If there were a large number of names, this could cause problems when trying to locate a client record.

Alphabetical sorting is very simple, using a built-in **sort tool**, which allows us to sort data alphabetically A to Z, or reversely Z to A. Numeric data, can also be sorted in ascending or descending order.

When we are doing a sort we have to identify and select the data which is to be sorted. It is very important that we include any associated data in the nearby columns within our selection.

In the above example, because the data in the month columns is specific to the individual clients, if we change the order of the clients, we must also change the order of the monthly data in the same way. This will happen automatically if we include the associated columns in our selection, before we select sort. In the image below, the data in all six columns is selected.

	A6	▼	⊙	f_x	Smiths Ltd		⊗

	A	B	C	D	E	F	G
1	Work bookings						
2							
3	Hourly rate	£20					
4							
5	Client	Month1	Month2	Month3	Month4	Total	
6	Smiths Ltd	15	15	15	15	60	
7	Jones and Partner	12	8	10	9	39	
8	Redwoods	13	20	11	7	51	
9	Underhills	13	20	11	2	46	

We then select **Sort and Filter** from the Home menu, choose order alphabetically A to Z and get the results below.

	A	B	C	D	E	F	G
	A6		▼	f_x	Jones and Partner		
1	Work bookings						
2							
3	Hourly rate	£20					
4							
5	Client	Month1	Month2	Month3	Month4	Total	
6	Jones and Partner	12	8	10	9	39	
7	Redwoods	13	20	11	7	51	
8	Smiths Ltd	15	15	15	15	60	
9	Underhills	13	20	11	2	46	
10							

You can see that all the data has moved with the individual client name and remains correct.

The data will always be sorted by the first column on the left, unless you use **Custom Sort**, and specifically choose a different column.

When doing a **sort** to a column containing text, we could chose reverse order Z to A if required.

Columns containing numbers can be sorted in **Ascending** (increasing) or **Descending** (decreasing) order.

In summary, to sort data:

■ **Select** the data which we want to sort (including any associated data)

■ Select **Sort and Filter** from the menu

■ Choose the **order** (A to Z, Z to A, Ascending or Descending) as appropriate

filter

If you have a spreadsheet containing a large amount of data as in the example below (which shows sales by month) the **Filter** facility allows you to filter the data so that you only see rows which contain certain values or combinations of values. For example **Filter** could show just those rows where Region=North West or a combination such as Region=North West and Manufacturer=Ford (see illustration on the next page).

	A	B	C	D	E	F
	G1	▾	fx			
1	Year	Month	Manufacturer	Type	Region	Quantity
2	2012	Feb	Ford	T	South	1,500
3	2012	Feb	Seat	I	East	220
4	2012	Mar	Seat	I	South West	155
5	2012	Apr	VW	O	North West	35
6	2012	Mar	Mercedes	M	North West	125
7	2012	Jan	BMW	T	South	126
8	2012	Mar	Toyota	I	East	45
9	2012	Jul	VW	O	South West	56
10	2012	Feb	Ford	O	South West	68
11	2012	Jan	Seat	M	South	100
12	2012	Apr	Seat	T	South	1,460
13	2012	Aug	VW	I	East	1,500
14	2013	Jan	Mercedes	I	South West	220

To **Filter** data:

■ place the cursor in the cell containing the leftmost heading text

■ select **Filter** from the **Sort and Filter** menu.

You will see something similar to the image below.

	A	B	C	D	E	F
1	Year ▾	Month ▾	Manufacturer ▾	Type ▾	Region ▾	Quanti ▾
2	2012	Feb	Ford	T	South	1,500
3	2012	Feb	Seat	I	East	220
4	2012	Mar	Seat	I	South West	155
5	2012	Apr	VW	O	North West	35
6	2012	Mar	Mercedes	M	North West	125
7	2012	Jan	BMW	T	South	126
8	2012	Mar	Toyota	I	East	45
9	2012	Jul	VW	O	South West	56

To filter the data:

■ click on the drop down arrow on a column

■ select the required values which you wish to analyse from the drop down menu

■ repeat on other columns as required to refine the rows displayed

⊿	A	B	C	D	E	F
1	Year ▾	Month ▾	Manufacturer ⌄T	Type ▾	Region ⌄T	Quantit ▾
25	2011	Apr	Ford	O	North West	56
33	2012	Dec	Ford	P	North West	34
40						
41						

The image above shows the rows displayed, when a filter of Region = North West, and Manufacturer = Ford has been applied.

To **Turn off** the active filter on a column:

- click on the Filter symbol on the column

- select clear filters

To **Remove all Filters**:

- select **Filter** from the **Sort and Filter** menu

(The filter icon will be highlighted in the menu, showing filtering is active.)

SUB TOTALS

There are usually facilities within the spreadsheet package to calculate subtotals or totals for sections of data within your worksheet.

For example, when we were looking at a book sales worksheet, we wanted to total the sales of a particular book, as shown in the example below.

C13	▾	f_x	=C4+C11		�˅
⊿	A	B	C	D	E
2					
3	**Book**	**Author**	**Quantity**		
4	Lord of the Rings	Tolkien	10		
5	Pride and Prejudice	Austen	5		
6	Far from the Madding Crowd	Hardy	8		
7	Oliver Twist	Dickens	3		
8	Wuthering Heights	Bronte	6		
9	Oliver Twist	Dickens	2		
10	Pride and Prejudice	Austen	2		
11	Lord of the Rings	Tolkien	2		
12					
13	Lord of the Rings	Sales	12		
14	Oliver Twist	Sales	5		

In this case we created a formula to add up the specific rows for the relevant books, as seen by the formula in cell C13 which adds up cells C4 and C11 to produce a **Subtotal** for sales of *Lord of the Rings*. It is possible for the spreadsheet package to do all this for us.

The first step is to order/sort the data, so that it is arranged by the column for which we want subtotals. For example, if we want subtotals by book title we will sort the data by that column, if we want subtotals by author, we would sort the data by that column.

Let us assume we want to create **Sub totals by author**, ie we want to know how many books by each author have been sold. We will first sort the data as shown below, using Custom Sort, and selecting the **Author column**. The data is then shown in alphabetical order by Author.

	A	B	C	D	E
1	**Summer sales**				
2					
3	**Book**	**Author**	**Quantity**		
4	Pride and Prejudice	Austen	5		
5	Pride and Prejudice	Austen	2		
6	Wuthering Heights	Bronte	6		
7	Oliver Twist	Dickens	3		
8	Oliver Twist	Dickens	2		
9	Far from the Madding Crowd	Hardy	8		
10	Lord of the Rings	Tolkien	10		
11	Lord of the Rings	Tolkien	2		

The next step is to select all the data including our column headings, and select **Subtotal** from the **Data** menu bar.

The Subtotal options then appear, and we have to make some choices:

1   The first choice is the column for which we need a subtotal.

The default choice is the column on the left – the 'Book' column.

Because we want to create a Subtotal for each author, we use the 'Author' column. For **At each change in** we select 'Author'.

2   The next choice is the **function** we want to use.

We select **SUM**, because we want to total the number of books sold by each author.

3   The final choice is the column we are adding up and the column to which we want to add a Subtotal.

We select the Quantity column.

4   You should keep the defaults for the remaining options.

The results are shown in the screen below.

	A	B	C	D
1	**Summer sales**			
2				
3	Book	Author	Quantity	
4	Pride and Prejudice	Austen	5	
5	Pride and Prejudice	Austen	2	
6		**Austen Total**	7	
7	Wuthering Heights	Bronte	6	
8		**Bronte Total**	6	
9	Oliver Twist	Dickens	3	
10	Oliver Twist	Dickens	2	
11		**Dickens Total**	5	
12	Far from the Madding Crowd	Hardy	8	
13		**Hardy Total**	8	
14	Lord of the Rings	Tolkien	10	
15	Lord of the Rings	Tolkien	2	
16		**Tolkien Total**	12	
17		**Grand Total**	38	

Looking at the image above, on the left hand side, you can see minus (-) symbols and lines, these are known as **outlines**, which allow us to see all the **detail** rows making up the subtotals.

We can chose to just see the summary of subtotals in outline, either by selecting individual minus (-) symbols on the left or selecting all the data, and then **Hide Detail** from the menu. As shown in the image below, you can see that the minus signs are now replaced by plus signs (+).

1 2 3		A	B	C	D	E
	1	**Summer sales**				
	2					
	3	Book	Author	Quantity		
+	6		Austen Total	7		
+	8		Bronte Total	6		
+	11		Dickens Total	5		
+	13		Hardy Total	8		
+	16		Tolkien Total	12		
−	17		Grand Total	38		

Sheet1 **Sales** Sheet3

As you can see from the screens on the previous page and above, the Subtotal function is extremely useful when we have large amounts of data, and only want to look at a summary.

If you need to revert to full detail, either select individual plus signs (+), or select all the data and then show detail from the menu.

LINKING AND EMBEDDING

The terms **linking and embedding** – also known as **OLE** (Object Linking and Embedding) – are used to describe a technique where data created by one software package is inserted into a file created by another software package.

For example we might want to **place data from a spreadsheet into a word processing document**.

There are several ways of doing this:

■ simple **Copy and Paste**

■ **Embedding**

■ **Linking**

copy and paste

Copy and Paste would just put a copy of the spreadsheet data in the word processing document, but if anything changed in the original spreadsheet, the data would not change in the document.

embedding

If we **Embed** the data in the word processing document, it creates a static copy of the spreadsheet data as a table in the word processing document, so if anything changed in the original spreadsheet, the data would not change in the document. This can be useful if you don't want the document to reflect changes in the spreadsheet.

If you select to edit this table of spreadsheet data within the word processing document (usually by DOUBLE CLICK), it will automatically open up the spreadsheet software and display the data ready to be changed.

To insert spreadsheet data as embedded:

Select and copy the data in the original spreadsheet, switch to the word processing package with the document open, select **Paste Special**, and paste as a worksheet object.

linking

If the spreadsheet data were **linked** in the word processing document, then if it changed in the original spreadsheet, it would automatically update in the word processing document the next time the word processing document was opened, or if it were open when the original spreadsheet were changed.

To link data:

First select the data in the original worksheet to copy, switch to the word processing package with a document open, select **Paste Special**, paste as a worksheet object, and select **Paste Link**.

This is an area where you should experiment with your software packages, since detailed key strokes will vary from package to package.

EXPORT AND IMPORT

In this section we will be looking at the concepts of importing and exporting text files.

Historically, if you wanted to move data from one software package to another, and the software packages were produced by different companies, you would take the data out of the first package – **export** – into a text file format, and then load or **import** the data as a text file into the second package.

The need to export and import has greatly reduced as software packages have become more sophisticated; however you may still need to do it.

There are two commonly used text files formats:

- **Delimited text files** (.txt), in which the TAB character typically separates each field of text.

- **Comma separated values** text files (.csv), in which the comma character (,) typically separates each field of text.

An example csv file based on the book sales spreadsheet is shown below.

```
Summer sales,,
,,
Book,Author,Quantity
Pride and Prejudice,Austen,5
Pride and Prejudice,Austen,2
Wuthering Heights,Bronte,6
Oliver Twist,Dickens,3
Oliver Twist,Dickens,2
Far from the Madding Crowd,Hardy,8
Lord of the Rings,Tolkien,10
Lord of the Rings,Tolkien,2
```

You can see each cell of data is separated by a comma, and each row of data is output on a fresh line. The lines with no data, just commas, are our blank lines within the spreadsheet, and are included for consistency.

To export data from a spreadsheet:

- Select **Save as** from the menu

- From the **Format** or **Save as type** select **Text** (tab delimited), or **CSV** (comma separated)

- Select the folder and specify the file name where you wish to store the file

Note that only the current worksheet will be exported from a workbook, and formatting will generally not be carried through into the text file.

To import the data to create a spreadsheet:

- Select **Open** from the menu

- From the **Files of type** select **Text** files

- Select the folder and the file name to import

- Save the file using **Save as** from the File menu and select a **File type of spreadsheet** from the drop-down list of file types.

Chapter Summary

In this chapter we have covered the following spreadsheet concepts and techniques:

- formula validation

- spell check

- find and replace

- sorting and filtering data

- introducing subtotals

- linking and embedding

- exporting and importing data

You should now carry out some or all of the exercises on the next few pages in order to practise and reinforce your learning.

Exercise 1 – validating formulas and spell check

In this first exercise we are going to practise using the tools available for validating formulas and checking the spelling of our text, using a spreadsheet already created. We will then create a new spreadsheet.

To download the spreadsheet which has already been created visit www.osbornebooks.co.uk ('Resources'). The filename is **T5investcheck.** This spreadsheet sets out the interest (or gain) and the growth obtained from a variety of investments over different time periods.

Stage 1

This stage covers checking the formulas in our spreadsheet.

1. Download the workbook **T5investcheck**

2. Open the downloaded file, **Save** the workbook with new name **T5Exercise1**

    The workbook should be familiar from the exercises in Topic 4, it should appear as shown below.

	A	B	C	D	E	F	G
1	Investment Portfolio						
2					Annual	Weekly	
3		Year start	Year end	Interest or	Growth	Growth	Maximum
4	Where	Amount	Amount	Gain	Rate	Amount	Growth
5		£	£	£	%	£	£
6	Bank1	£500	£512.50	£12.50	2.50%	£0.24	£100.77
7	Bank2	£4,000	£4,100.33	£100.33	2.51%	£1.93	£403.08
8	Building Society1	£2,000	£2,100.00	£100.00	5.00%	£1.92	£403.08
9	Building Society2	£3,000	£3,099.99	£99.99	3.33%	£1.92	£604.62
10	Post Office	£100	£102.95	£2.95	2.95%	£0.06	£20.15
11	Stocks & shares	£1,000	£1,201.54	£201.54	20.15%	£3.88	£33.33
12	Totals	£9,600	£9,916				

3. From the menu, select **Options, Formulas.** Change if necessary so that background error checking is off. (This is useful for this stage of the exercise)

4. As a first step to validation, select **Show Formulas** from the menu bar. See if you can see any errors in the formulas – do not make any changes.

5. Move from formula to formula and you will see the cells making up that formula highlighted. Where you think there may be an error, change the font to show red, but do not change the formula yet.

6. Select **Show Formulas** again, so the formulas are now hidden.

7. Select **Options, Formulas**, and change **Background Error Checking** to **On**. You should now see some green error triangles appear in the top left-hand corner of those cells which may contain an error. These should coincide with those cells which you changed to a red font.

8. Select **Error Checking** from the menu bar. Follow the process as it steps through each cell. Where it identifies a possible error, change as appropriate.

9. Save the workbook with the same name **T5Exercise1**

   It should have the same values as the image shown below

	A	B	C	D	E	F	G
1	Investment Portfolio						
2					Annual	Weekly	
3		Year start	Year end	Interest or	Growth	Growth	Maximum
4	Where	Amount	Amount	Gain	Rate	Amount	Growth
5		£	£	£	%	£	£
6	Bank1	£500	£512.50	£12.50	2.50%	£0.24	£100.77
7	Bank2	£4,000	£4,100.33	£100.33	2.51%	£1.93	£806.16
8	Building Society1	£2,000	£2,100.00	£100.00	*5.00%*	£1.92	£403.08
9	Building Society2	£3,000	£3,099.99	£99.99	*3.33%*	£1.92	£604.62
10	Post Office	£100	£102.95	£2.95	2.95%	£0.06	£20.15
11	Stocks & shares	£1,000	£1,201.54	£201.54	*20.15%*	£3.88	£33.33
12	Totals	£10,600	£11,117				

10. Check that your values match. If they do not, you should step through the error checking routine again and correct formulas as appropriate.

11. Select **Show Formulas** so that all formulas are displayed. The corrected worksheet should look as shown below. (The columns have been narrowed for the purpose of the illustration.)

	A	B	C	D	E	F	G
1	Investment Portf						
2					Annual	Weekly	
3		Year start	Year end	Interest or	Growth	Growth	Maximum
4	Where	Amount	Amount	Gain	Rate	Amount	Growth
5		£	£	£	%	£	£
6	Bank1	500	512.5	=C6-B6	=D6/B6	=D6/52	=B6*$E$11
7	Bank2	4000	4100.33	=C7-B7	=D7/B7	=D7/52	=B7*$E$11
8	Building Society1	2000	2100	=C8-B8	*=D8/B8*	=D8/52	=B8*$E$11
9	Building Society2	3000	3099.99	=C9-B9	*=D9/B9*	=D9/52	=B9*$E$11
10	Post Office	100	102.95	=C10-B10	=D10/B10	=D10/52	=B10*$E$11
11	Stocks & shares	1000	1201.54	201.54	*=D11/B11*	=D11/52	=B11*E9
12	Totals	=SUM(B6:B11)	=SUM(C6:C11)				
13							

Stage 2

In this stage, we are going to continue checking the formulas in the Investment Portfolio spreadsheet.

1. Change the value in cell C9 to £3,300.

2. Look how this affects the Maximum Growth (cell G11) for Stocks & shares.

3. Select cell G11, select **Trace Precedents**.

4. Select G6, select **Trace Precedents**.

5. Select G7 Select, select **Trace Precedents**

6. Select G8, select **Trace Precedents**.

You can see from this that a pattern emerges:

Cells G6, G7, G8 all use cell E11 in their formula, but cell G11 does not. This is an error which was not picked up by the error checking facility, although it did find several other errors as we saw earlier. The process is not foolproof.

The worksheet should look as shown in the image below.

	A	B	C	D	E	F	G
1	Investment Portfolio						
2					Annual	Weekly	
3		Year start	Year end	Interest or	Growth	Growth	Maximum
4	Where	Amount	Amount	Gain	Rate	Amount	Growth
5		£	£	£	%	£	£
6	Bank1	£500	£512.50	£12.50	2.50%	£0.24	£100.77
7	Bank2	£4,000	£4,100.33	£100.33	2.51%	£1.93	£806.16
8	Building Society1	£2,000	£2,100.00	£100.00	5.00%	£1.92	£403.08
9	Building Society2	£3,000	£3,300.00	£300.00	10.00%	£5.77	£604.62
10	Post Office	£100	£102.95	£2.95	2.95%	£0.06	£20.15
11	Stocks & shares	£1,000	£1,201.54	£201.54	20.15%	£3.88	£100.00
12	Totals	£10,600	£11,317				

7. Select **Remove Arrows**, to clear all arrows from the worksheet.

8. Select cell E11, select **Trace Dependents**.

9. Select cell E9, select **Trace Dependents**.

You can see from the arrows, as shown in the image at the top of the next page, that the formula in cell G11 is incorrectly dependent on cell E9.

	A	B	C	D	E	F	G
1	Investment Portfolio						
2					Annual	Weekly	
3		Year start	Year end	Interest or	Growth	Growth	Maximum
4	Where	Amount	Amount	Gain	Rate	Amount	Growth
5		£	£	£	%	£	£
6	Bank1	£500	£512.50	£12.50	2.50%	£0.24	£100.77
7	Bank2	£4,000	£4,100.33	£100.33	2.51%	£1.93	£806.16
8	Building Society1	£2,000	£2,100.00	£100.00	5.00%	£1.92	£403.08
9	Building Society2	£3,000	£3,300.00	£300.00	10.00%	£5.77	£604.62
10	Post Office	£100	£102.95	£2.95	2.95%	£0.06	£20.15
11	Stocks & shares	£1,000	£1,201.54	£201.54	20.15%	£3.88	£100.00
12	Totals	£10,600	£11,317				

10. Correct the formula in cell G11.

11. Select cell D11, select **Trace Precedents**.

   You will receive an error message to say that this cell does not contain a formula. This highlights that there is something wrong, because it should contain a formula.

12. Enter £1,350 in cell C11. See how cell D11 does not change. Enter the appropriate formula in D11 and see how all the values in column G now update.

   Your spreadsheet should now look as shown below.

	A	B	C	D	E	F	G
1	Investment Portfolio						
2					Annual	Weekly	
3		Year start	Year end	Interest or	Growth	Growth	Maximum
4	Where	Amount	Amount	Gain	Rate	Amount	Growth
5		£	£	£	%	£	£
6	Bank1	£500	£512.50	£12.50	2.50%	£0.24	£175.00
7	Bank2	£4,000	£4,100.33	£100.33	2.51%	£1.93	£1,400.00
8	Building Society1	£2,000	£2,100.00	£100.00	5.00%	£1.92	£700.00
9	Building Society2	£3,000	£3,300.00	£300.00	10.00%	£5.77	£1,050.00
10	Post Office	£100	£102.95	£2.95	2.95%	£0.06	£35.00
11	Stocks & shares	£1,000	£1,350.00	£350.00	35.00%	£6.73	£350.00
12	Totals	£10,600	£11,466				

13. Save the workbook with the name **T5Exercise1**

   You have now completed the first exercise.

Exercise 2 – using spell check and search and replace

In this next exercise we are going to use the built in spell check facility and search and replace to make corrections and changes to text within our worksheet. We are again going to make use of an existing spreadsheet which contains data relating to international sales of fashion items.

This spreadsheet contains nearly 40 rows of data relating to sales information: the month of the sale, the category of product, the value, the sales rep that made the sale and the country to which the sale was made. Not all 40 rows will be visible at the same time on the screen images in this book.

To download this sales spreadsheet visit www.osbornebooks.co.uk ('Resources'). The filename is **T5sales**

Stage 1

This stage uses the built in spell check tool within a previously created workbook.

1.   Download the workbook **T5sales**

2.   Open the downloaded file, save the workbook with new name **T5Exercise2**. The workbook should appear as shown below.

	A	B	C	D	E	F	G
1	Sales						
2							
3	Month	Product	Value	Sales Rep	Country		
4	Jan	Acessories	£125.75	TP	UK		
5	Jan	Footwear	£99.95	SM	UK		
6	Jan	Lugage	£220.00	py	ger		
7	Feb	Jewelery	£1,500.00	TP	UK		
8	Feb	Footwear	£220.00	py	Fr		
9	Feb	Jewelery	£67.75	IO	ger		
10	Feb	Clothing	£34.90	SM	Sp		
11	Mar	Footwear	£154.50	py	ger		
12	Mar	Lugage	£124.60	SM	Sp		
13	Mar	Clothing	£44.75	py	Fr		

Sheet1 / Sheet2 / Sheet3

3.   Select cells B4 to B10 in the Product column.

4.   Select the **Spell check** option from the menu.

5.   Step through the individual checks, making corrections as appropriate, choosing the correct spelling from the choices offered.

6.   Select the whole of column B (using the column header).

7.   Select the **Spell check** option from the menu.

8.   Step through the individual checks, choosing the correct spelling from the choices offered, and this time select **Change All**, to correct all occurrences in column B which are spelt incorrectly.

9.   Save the workbook with the name **T5Exercise2**

Your spreadsheet should now look as shown below:-

	A	B	C	D	E	F	G
1	Sales						
2							
3	Month	Product	Value	Sales Rep	Country		
4	Jan	Accessories	£125.75	TP	UK		
5	Jan	Footwear	£99.95	SM	UK		
6	Jan	Luggage	£220.00	py	ger		
7	Feb	Jewellery	£1,500.00	TP	UK		
8	Feb	Footwear	£220.00	py	Fr		
9	Feb	Jewellery	£67.75	IO	ger		
10	Feb	Clothing	£34.90	SM	Sp		
11	Mar	Footwear	£154.50	py	ger		
12	Mar	Luggage	£124.60	SM	Sp		
13	Mar	Clothing	£44.75	py	Fr		

Sheet1 / Sheet2 / Sheet3

Stage 2

We are going to use the **Find** facility to locate some specific values, and also the **Find and Replace** to make some more changes to the data.

1.   In the Value column (column C) we have a query regarding a sale of value £67.75 where Country (column E) is UK. Use the **Find** facility to find this entry, selecting next until you find the required row, and change the text font style to Italics for this row of data.

2.   Use the **Find** facility to find the month Nov (column A), where Product (column B) is **Other**. Change the text font style to Bold for this row of data. Note that this entry may not initially be visible on your screen due to the number of rows of data in this worksheet.

3.   Use the **Find and Replace** facility to change all occurrences of py in the Sales Rep column (column D) to all capitals – PY.

4.   Use the **Find and Replace** facility to change all occurrences of Fr in the Country column (column E) to all capitals – FR.

5.   Again, in the Country column (column E), change all occurrences of ger, and Sp to all capitals GER and SP.

6.   Save the workbook with the name **T5Exercise2**

Your spreadsheet should appear as shown in the image on the next page.

	A	B	C	D	E	F	G
1	Sales						
2							
3	Month	Product	Value	Sales Rep	Country		
4	Jan	Accessories	£125.75	TP	UK		
5	Jan	Footwear	£99.95	SM	UK		
6	Jan	Luggage	£220.00	PY	GER		
7	Feb	Jewellery	£1,500.00	TP	UK		
8	Feb	Footwear	£220.00	PY	FR		
9	Feb	Jewellery	£67.75	IO	GER		
10	Feb	Clothing	£34.90	SM	SP		
11	Mar	Footwear	£154.50	PY	GER		
12	Mar	Luggage	£124.60	SM	SP		
13	Mar	Clothing	£44.75	PY	FR		

Sheet1 / Sheet2 / Sheet3

The image below shows the rows with the different font styles.

Note that Row 27 is now in italics and Row 38 is in Bold.

	A	B	C	D	E	F	G
27	*Aug*	*Luggage*	*£67.75*	*SM*	*UK*		
28	Aug	Clothing	£99.95	TP	UK		
29	Aug	Other	£1,460.40	PY	FR		
30	Sep	Accessories	£1,460.40	PY	FR		
31	Sep	Accessories	£34.00	PY	GER		
32	Sep	Clothing	£154.50	SM	UK		
33	Oct	Accessories	£67.75	IO	GER		
34	Oct	Clothing	£99.95	SM	UK		
35	Oct	Accessories	£34.90	PY	GER		
36	Nov	Footwear	£124.60	SM	SP		
37	Nov	Footwear	£125.75	TP	UK		
38	**Nov**	**Other**	**£44.75**	**PY**	**FR**		
39	Nov	Accessories	£56.00	PY	FR		

Sheet1 / Sheet2 / Sheet3

You have now completed the second exercise.

Exercise 3 – using Subtotals

In this next exercise we are going to use sorting and introduce some Subtotals. We will use the workbook from the previous exercise.

This workbook can be downloaded from www.osbornebooks.co.uk ('Resources'), filename **T5sort**

Stage 1

In this stage we are going to use the **Sort** facility.

Note: one facility which you may need to make use of, which is common to all packages, is the **Undo** button or option. This will allow you to revert the data back a step at a time, undoing your changes or edits. This is particularly useful when doing a sort, since if you sort incorrectly and mix up the data, there is no other easy way to get back to where you were before you started to sort the data.

1.   Either open your workbook **T5Exercise2**, or download the workbook **T5sort**.

2.   Save the workbook with new name **T5Exercise3**

The workbook should look as shown below:

	A	B	C	D	E	F	G
1	Sales						
2							
3	Month	Product	Value	Sales Rep	Country		
4	Jan	Accessories	£125.75	TP	UK		
5	Jan	Footwear	£99.95	SM	UK		
6	Jan	Luggage	£220.00	PY	GER		
7	Feb	Jewellery	£1,500.00	TP	UK		
8	Feb	Footwear	£220.00	PY	FR		
9	Feb	Jewellery	£67.75	IO	GER		
10	Feb	Clothing	£34.90	SM	SP		
11	Mar	Footwear	£154.50	PY	GER		
12	Mar	Luggage	£124.60	SM	SP		
13	Mar	Clothing	£44.75	PY	FR		

Sheet1 Sheet2 Sheet3

3.   We are going to sort the data by Product (column B). Select all the data and **Sort** alphabetically A -> Z.

Your spreadsheet should appear like the screen image at the top of the next page.

	A	B	C	D	E	F	G
1	Sales						
2							
3	Month	Product	Value	Sales Rep	Country		
4	Jan	Accessories	£125.75	TP	UK		
5	Mar	Accessories	£154.50	IO	SP		
6	May	Accessories	£144.50	IO	SP		
7	Jul	Accessories	£44.75	IO	GER		
8	Sep	Accessories	£1,460.40	PY	FR		
9	Sep	Accessories	£34.00	PY	GER		
10	Oct	Accessories	£67.75	IO	GER		
11	Oct	Accessories	£34.90	PY	GER		
12	Nov	Accessories	£56.00	PY	FR		
13	Dec	Accessories	£124.60	MP	GER		

Sheet1 Sheet2 Sheet3

4.   We now want to sort the data by value (column C) in descending order (largest to smallest).

Your spreadsheet should appear as shown in the image below:

	A	B	C	D	E	F	G
1	Sales						
2							
3	Month	Product	Value	Sales Rep	Country		
4	Feb	Jewellery	£1,500.00	TP	UK		
5	Aug	Other	£1,500.00	PY	FR		
6	Dec	Other	£1,500.00	IO	FR		
7	Sep	Accessories	£1,460.40	PY	FR		
8	Apr	Footwear	£1,460.40	TP	UK		
9	Aug	Other	£1,460.40	PY	FR		
10	Jun	Clothing	£1,124.60	TP	UK		
11	May	Other	£344.90	IO	SP		
12	Feb	Footwear	£220.00	PY	FR		
13	Jan	Luggage	£220.00	PY	GER		
14	Nov	Luggage	£220.00	IO	SP		

Sheet1 Sheet2 Sheet3

5. Save the workbook with the name **T5Exercise3**

Stage 2

We are now going to introduce some subtotals. We want to subtotal the value of sales by Sales Rep.

1.   **Sort** the data by the Sales Rep (column D). **Sort** alphabetically A -> Z.

2.   Using the **Subtotal** facility, we want to subtotal at each change of Sales Rep. Use function **SUM**, add subtotal to **Value**, **Replace** current subtotals (yes), summary below data (yes).

3.   Select the **Hide Detail** option from the menu bar.

4.   Widen the value column so that all data displays in full.

5.   Save the workbook with the name **T5Exercise3a**

Your spreadsheet should appear as shown in the image below.

1 2 3		A	B	C	D	E	F
	3	Month	Product	Value	Sales Rep	Country	
+	17			£2,803.80	IO Total		
+	20			£158.60	MP Total		
+	33			£5,355.45	PY Total		
+	41			£706.25	SM Total		
+	49			£4,561.05	TP Total		
−	50			£13,585.15	Grand Total		
	51						

6.   Select the IO total row (row 17), and either click on the plus sign (+) to the left of the row, or select the **Show Detail** option from the menu bar.

Your spreadsheet should appear as shown in the image below.

1 2 3		A	B	C	D	E	F
·	4	Dec	Other	£1,500.00	IO	FR	
·	5	May	Other	£344.90	IO	SP	
·	6	Nov	Luggage	£220.00	IO	SP	
·	7	Mar	Accessories	£154.50	IO	SP	
·	8	May	Accessories	£144.50	IO	SP	
·	9	Oct	Accessories	£67.75	IO	GER	
·	10	Feb	Jewellery	£67.75	IO	GER	
·	11	Dec	Luggage	£56.25	IO	GER	
·	12	Apr	Other	£56.25	IO	GER	
·	13	Jul	Other	£56.25	IO	GER	
·	14	Apr	Jewellery	£56.00	IO	SP	
·	15	Jul	Accessories	£44.75	IO	GER	
·	16	Apr	Other	£34.90	IO	SP	
−	17			£2,803.80	IO Total		
+	20			£158.60	MP Total		
+	33			£5,355.45	PY Total		
+	41			£706.25	SM Total		
+	49			£4,561.05	TP Total		
−	50			£13,585.15	Grand Total		

Stage 3

We are now going to use this same data to practise using the **Filter** tool.

1. Open the copy of the workbook which you saved with the name **T5Exercise3** or download the workbook **T5sort**.

2. Select the **filter** tool to apply a filter.

3. On the Country column, apply a filter so that you can only see rows where Country is GER.

The workbook should look as shown below.

	A	B	C	D	E	F
1	Sales					
2						
3	Month ▼	Product ▼	Value ▼	Who ▼	Countr ⊤	
6	Mar	Footwear	£154.50	IY	GER	
11	Jul	Other	£56.25	IO	GER	
12	Feb	Jewellery	£67.75	IO	GER	
16	Jan	Luggage	£220.00	IY	GER	
21	Jul	Accessories	£44.75	IO	GER	
22	Apr	Other	£56.25	IO	GER	
26	Sep	Accessories	£34.00	IY	GER	
31	Dec	Luggage	£56.25	IO	GER	
32	Oct	Accessories	£67.75	IO	GER	
40	Oct	Accessories	£34.90	IY	GER	
41	Dec	Accessories	£124.60	MP	GER	

4.   Apply an additional filter to the rows, using the product column, so that only the rows for Product = Accessories and Country = GER are to be shown.

The workbook should look as shown below. This completes Exercise 3.

	A	B	C	D	E
1	Sales				
2					
3	Month ▾	Product ▾	Value ▾	Who ▾	Countr ▾
21	Jul	Accessories	£44.75	IO	GER
26	Sep	Accessories	£34.00	IY	GER
32	Oct	Accessories	£67.75	IO	GER
40	Oct	Accessories	£34.90	IY	GER
41	Dec	Accessories	£124.60	MP	GER
42					

Exercise 4 – embedding, linking, importing and exporting data

In this exercise we are going to practise linking and embedding, and explore the import and export facilities. We will be using a word processing document, and a workbook containing the required spreadsheet data

If necessary, the following files can be downloaded from www.osbornebooks.co.uk ('Resources'): filename **T5embed** (the workbook), and **T5word** (a word processing document in Microsoft® Word format).

Stage 1

This stage uses **embedding** with a previously created workbook.

1. Open **T5embed** in your spreadsheet program, and **T5word**d in your word processing package.

    The word processing file should look as shown below:

This document is to be used as a test document for linking or embedding information from a spreadsheet.

Insert your embedded warehouse data here.

Insert your linked warehouse data here

The workbook should appear as follows:

	A	B	C	D
1	Warehouse information			
2				
3				
4	Code	Bin	Price	
5	ab1	1	£2.00	
6	ab2	2	£30.00	
7	ab3	1	£27.00	
8	ab4	1	£14.00	
9	ab5	3	£21.00	
10	ab6	4	£12.00	
11	ab7	1	£7.00	
12	ab8	2	£24.00	
13	ab9	1	£27.00	
14	ab10	5	£50.00	

2. Within the open worksheet, select all cells in the range A4:C14. Select **Copy** from the Edit menu, or use **CTRL** and **C** to copy the data.

3. Turning to the word processing package, move down the document, so that the cursor is below the text relating to embedding the data. Select **Paste Special**, and paste as worksheet object.

The document should appear as follows:

This document is to be used as a test document for linking or embedding information from a spreadsheet.

Insert your embedded warehouse data here.

Code	Bin	Price
ab1	1	£2.00
ab2	2	£30.00
ab3	1	£27.00
ab4	1	£14.00
ab5	3	£21.00
ab6	4	£12.00
ab7	1	£7.00

4. Stay in the word processing package, double click on the inserted data, and change the price for **ab1** to **£2.50**. Return to the word processing document.

5. Save the word processing document as **T5word5**

Stage 2

This stage uses linking to connect a word processing file with a previously created workbook.

1. If the files are not already open, open the word processing package, with file **T5word5**, and open the spreadsheet with workbook **T5embed**.

2. Within the open worksheet, select all cells in the range A4:C14, select **Copy** from the Edit menu, or use **CTRL** and **C** to copy the data.

3. Turning to the word processing package, move down the document, so that the cursor is below the text relating to linking the data, select **Paste Special**, **Paste as Worksheet Object**, and select **Paste Link**.

The document should appear as shown at the top of the next page.

Insert your linked warehouse data here

Code	Bin	Price
ab1	1	£2.00
ab2	2	£30.00
ab3	1	£27.00
ab4	1	£14.00
ab5	3	£21.00
ab6	4	£12.00
ab7	1	£7.00
ab8	2	£24.00
ab9	1	£27.00
ab10	5	£50.00

4. Remain in the word processing package, double click on the inserted data, which will take you to the spreadsheet package, change the price for **ab1** to **£2.50**, swap back to the word processing package, select the linked data table, and select **Update Link**, if it has not automatically updated.

5. Swap to the spreadsheet package, change cell C8 to **£16**, swap back to the word processing document, select the linked data table, and select **Update Link** if it has not automatically updated.

6. Save the word processing document as **T5word5**

    The document should appear as shown below.

    You can see in the linked data section of this word processing document that the price for **ab1** has also been updated to **£2.50**, without you having to edit it.

Insert your linked warehouse data here

Code	Bin	Price
ab1	1	£2.50
ab2	2	£30.00
ab3	1	£27.00
ab4	1	£16.00
ab5	3	£21.00
ab6	4	£12.00
ab7	1	£7.00
ab8	2	£24.00
ab9	1	£27.00
ab10	5	£50.00

Stage 3

In this stage we will use the **Save As** facility within the spreadsheet package to allow us to take an existing worksheet and **export** it to produce a text file containing the spreadsheet data, in the form of a .TXT or .CSV file

The file **T5export** can be downloaded from www.osbornebooks.co.uk.

1. Download and open **T5export** in your spreadsheet program.

    The workbook should appear as shown below.

	A	B	C	D	E
1	Code	Bin	Price		
2	ab1	1	£2.50		
3	ab2	2	£30.00		
4	ab3	1	£27.00		
5	ab4	1	£16.00		
6	ab5	3	£21.00		
7	ab6	4	£12.00		
8	ab7	1	£7.00		
9	ab8	2	£24.00		
10	ab9	1	£27.00		
11	ab10	5	£50.00		

2. **Export** the spreadsheet as a Text (Tab delimited file), with name **T5txt**.

3. Open the file **T5txt** in Microsoft® Notepad or equivalent file (found from the **Start Menu**, under **All Programs, Accessories, Notepad**.)

    The file should appear as shown at the top of the next page.

4. Export the spreadsheet as a CSV (Comma delimited file), with name **T5csv**.

5. Open the file **T5csv** in Microsoft® Notepad (found from the **Start menu**, under **All Programs, Accessories, Notepad**). You will need to select **File Type – all files**.

    The file should appear as shown in the second image down on the next page.

text (tab delimited) file

```
Code      Bin       Price
ab1       1         £2.50
ab2       2         £30.00
ab3       1         £27.00
ab4       1         £16.00
ab5       3         £21.00
ab6       4         £12.00
ab7       1         £7.00
ab8       2         £24.00
ab9       1         £27.00
ab10      5         £50.00
```

CSV file

```
Code,Bin,Price
ab1,1,£2.50
ab2,2,£30.00
ab3,1,£27.00
ab4,1,£16.00
ab5,3,£21.00
ab6,4,£12.00
ab7,1,£7.00
ab8,2,£24.00
ab9,1,£27.00
ab10,5,£50.00
```

Stage 4

In this stage we will **import** the spreadsheet data held in the text file which we have previously exported in Stage 3, and use it to create a new copy of the original spreadsheet.

1. Open your spreadsheet program.

2. Select **File**, **Open**, change **Files of Type** to **All Files**, select the file **T5txt**.

3. Step through the import options, make sure the **File Origin** is **Windows (ANSI)**. On Step 2 of 3, the Delimiters, make sure the **Tab** box is checked.

    The workbook should appear as shown at the top of the next page.

	A	B	C	D	E
1	Code	Bin	Price		
2	ab1	1	£2.50		
3	ab2	2	£30.00		
4	ab3	1	£27.00		
5	ab4	1	£16.00		
6	ab5	3	£21.00		
7	ab6	4	£12.00		
8	ab7	1	£7.00		
9	ab8	2	£24.00		
10	ab9	1	£27.00		
11	ab10	5	£50.00		

Note how all the formatting we had for our column headings has been stripped out of the data.

4. Save the spreadsheet data which is displayed, as **File type Spreadsheet**, and name it **T5ex4txt**

5. Still with the spreadsheet package open, select **File**, **Open**, change **Files of Type** to **All Files**. Select the file **T5csv**.

There are no import options this time, but you can see that the formatting has again been stripped out of the data, but the results are exactly the same.

6. Save the spreadsheet data which is below, as **File Type Spreadsheet**, and name it **T5ex4csv**

	A	B	C	D	E
1	Code	Bin	Price		
2	ab1	1	£2.50		
3	ab2	2	£30.00		
4	ab3	1	£27.00		
5	ab4	1	£16.00		
6	ab5	3	£21.00		
7	ab6	4	£12.00		
8	ab7	1	£7.00		
9	ab8	2	£24.00		
10	ab9	1	£27.00		
11	ab10	5	£50.00		

6 Statistical functions and charts

this chapter covers...

This chapter covers the use of statistical formulas, and charts. It explains and takes you through the concepts and techniques listed below.

By the time you have finished this chapter and carried out the exercises which follow, you should be able to produce spreadsheets which perform a variety of statistical calculations and create appropriate charts to illustrate worksheet data.

The concepts and techniques covered are:

- simple statistical functions

- analysis tools

- types of charts

- creating charts

Note that the the step-by-step instructions given in this chapter are based on the Microsoft ® Excel model, but the concepts and techniques described generally relate to all spreadsheet packages. The one exception to this is coverage of the Excel Data Analysis Toolpack in the section 'Analysis Tools'.

STATISTICAL FUNCTIONS

The functions we are going to cover in this chapter are as follows:

- COUNT
- MAX
- MIN
- AVERAGE

count

The **COUNT** function counts **the number of cells that contain numbers** within a group of cells specified by the user. The formula is:

=COUNT(value1,[value2],...)

The COUNT function has these arguments:

- **value1**

  This is required and can be the first item, cell reference, or range within which you want to count numbers

- **value2**

  This is optional.

You can specify up to 255 arguments. Each 'argument' can be either a number, cell reference, or range of cells.

Here are some examples:

=COUNT(B1:B16)

This would tell us how many cells in the range B1 to B16 contain numbers.

=COUNT(B1:B16,C20:C36)

This would return the total of how many cells in the range B1 to B16, and C20 to C36 contain numbers.

A simple illustration is shown in the screen image on the next page, where we are counting how many exam modules each college student took and record the result in a "Count" column.

We use the formula **=COUNT(B4:E4)** entered in F5 to tell us how many exams John Smith sat. This formula can then be copied to the remaining student rows.

A8		f_x	Barbara White			

	A	B	C	D	E	F	G
1	Midterm exams						
2							
3	Name	Module1	Module2	Module3	Module4	Count	
4	John Smith	75%	62%	45%	65%	4	
5	Harpret Bhopal	61%	48%			2	
6	Wendy Owen	63%	80%	51%	41%	4	
7	Mohammed Iqbal	53%		41%	64%	3	
8	Barbara White	42%	63%	85%	43%	4	
9							

Results / Sheet2 / Sheet3

MAX

'MAX' is an abbreviation of 'maximum'. The **MAX** function returns the maximum (largest) number within a group of cells specified by the user.

The formula is:

=MAX(number1,number2,...)

The **MAX** function has these arguments:

- **number1** – this is required

- **number2** – this is optional

You can specify up to 255 arguments for which you want to find the maximum value. Each argument can be either a number, cell reference, or range.

Here are some examples:

=MAX(B1:B6)

This would return the largest of the numbers in the range B1 to B6.

=MAX(B1:B6,80)

This would return the largest of the numbers in the range B1 to B6, and 80, ie if none of the numbers within the range is greater than 80 it would return a value of 80.

In the exam results spreadsheet shown on the next page, we have set up Row 10 to show the maximum (highest) mark for each of the four modules. the formula is input in B10 and copied to cells C10, D10 and E10.

B10	▼		f_x	=MAX(B4:B8)		
	A	B	C	D	E	F	G
1	Midterm exams						
2							
3	Name	Module1	Module2	Module3	Module4	Count	
4	John Smith	75%	62%	45%	65%	4	
5	Harpret Bhopal	61%	48%			2	
6	Wendy Owen	63%	80%	51%	41%	4	
7	Mohammed Iqbal	53%		41%	64%	3	
8	Barbara White	42%	63%	85%	43%	4	
9							
10	Max	75%	80%	85%	65%		
11							

Results / Sheet2 / Sheet3

MIN

'MIN' is an abbreviation of 'minimum'. The **MIN** function returns the smallest number within a group of cells specified by the user.

The formula is

> **=MIN(number1,number2,...)**

The **MIN** function has these arguments:

- **number1** – this is required

- **number2** – this is optional

You can specify up to 255 arguments for which you want to find the minimum value. Each argument can be either a number, or cell reference, or range.

Here are some examples:

> **=MIN(C2:C16)**

This would return the smallest of the numbers in the range C2 to C16.

> **=MIN(C2:C16,10)**

This would return the smallest of the numbers in the range C2 to C16, and 10, ie if none of the numbers within the range is smaller than 10 it would return a value of 10.

In the exam results spreadsheet shown on the next page, we have this time set up Row 10 to show the minimum (lowest) mark for each of the four modules. The formula has been input in B10 and copied to cells C10, D10 and E10.

	B10	▼	f_x	=MIN(B4:B8)		
	A	B	C	D	E	F	G
1	Midterm exams						
2							
3	**Name**	Module1	Module2	Module3	Module4	Count	
4	John Smith	75%	62%	45%	65%	4	
5	Harpret Bhopal	61%	48%			2	
6	Wendy Owen	63%	80%	51%	41%	4	
7	Mohammed Iqbal	53%		41%	64%	3	
8	Barbara White	42%	63%	85%	43%	4	
9							
10	Min	42%	48%	41%	41%		
11							

Results / Sheet2 / Sheet3 /

AVERAGE

The **AVERAGE** function returns the average (arithmetic mean) of a group of cells specified by the user.

The formula is:

=AVERAGE(number1,number2,...)

The **AVERAGE** function has these arguments:

■ **number1** – this is required

■ **number2** – this is optional

You can specify up to 255 arguments for which you want to find the **AVERAGE** value. Each argument can be either a number, or cell reference, or range.

Here are some examples:

= AVERAGE (C2:C16)

This would return the average of the numbers in the cell range C2 to C16.

= AVERAGE (C2:C16,10)

This would return the average of the numbers in the cell range C2 to C16 and 10.

In the example on the next page, the spreadsheet shows the time spent by a firm of accountants working for various clients – ie the time 'bookings'.

In this case we are finding out for Smiths Ltd the average time booked over a 5 week period. The formula used specifies the figures in row 4 as a range:

=AVERAGE(B4:F4)

	A	B	C	D	E	F	G
1	Work bookings						
2							
3	Client	Week1	Week2	Week3	Week4	Week5	Average
4	Smiths Ltd	15	20	15	20	15	17
5	Jones and Partner	12	8	10	9	9	
6	The Halal Centre	13	20	11	2	9	
7	Asian Foods	13	20	11	7	8	
8	Redwoods	0	19	12	5	12	
9	My Curries	2	14	0	12	0	

In the example below, we are using the same spreadsheet and working out the average time booked for Jones and Partner over the odd-numbered weeks, ie weeks 1, 3, and 5. The formula used is

=AVERAGE(B5,D5,F5)

G5				f_x	=AVERAGE(B5,D5,F5)		
	A	B	C	D	E	F	G
1	Work bookings						
2							
3	Client	Week1	Week2	Week3	Week4	Week5	Average
4	Smiths Ltd	15	20	15	20	15	17
5	Jones and Partner	12	8	10	9	9	10.33333333
6	The Halal Centre	13	20	11	2	9	
7	Asian Foods	13	20	11	7	8	
8	Redwoods	0	19	12	5	12	
9	My Curries	2	14	0	12	0	

ANALYSIS TOOLS

Tools for detailed statistical analysis may be provided within the spreadsheet program or package that you are using. The features will vary greatly from package to package. In this section we are going to describe and explain some of the tools available within the Microsoft ® Excel **Data Analysis Toolpak.**

We are not going to cover the statistical theory which underlies these tools, but will concentrate on how to use the functions provided by the tools.

We are going to describe:

- Rank and percentile

- Moving averages

- Histograms

The first step is to ensure that the Excel **Analysis Toolpak** has been loaded and is available. It is not loaded automatically by default at installation time.

To do this:

- select the **File** menu

- select **Options**

- select **Add-Ins**

- click on **Manage Add-Ins**

- click on **Go**

- ensure the box next to **Analysis ToolPak** is ticked by clicking in the box

If you cannot see **Analysis ToolPak** in the list of available Add-Ins, you will need to consult your system supervisor.

The list of available Add-Ins may look something like the image below, but will vary from computer to computer depending on what other software packages you have installed.

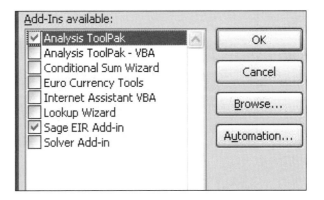

If **Analysis ToolPak** is not listed in the active Add-ins, or not 'ticked' in the list that appears, follow the installations steps for your particular version of Excel to install the **Analysis Toolpak**.

Once installation is complete, the tools can be accessed either from the **Tools** menu, or under the **Data** tab, depending on your version of Excel.

rank and percentile

The **rank and percentile** analysis tool produces a table that contains the **ordinal** and **percentage rank** of each value in a data set.

The **ordinal** is the ranking of each piece of data or number within the group of data, so the largest number within the group would be ranked 1, the second largest 2 and so on.

The **percentage** rank tells us what percentage of the remaining data values are less than this value. Therefore the value ranked 1 (the highest), will have a percentage rank of 100% since all other values are smaller than this one, and so on down the values order in descending order.

The best way to see how to use this tool is through an example.

If we look at the image below, we have a range of data values in column A.

	A	B	C	D	E	F	G	H
2	**Value**							
3	0.104							
4	0.247							
5	0.872							
6	1.47							
7	2.62							
8	3.96							
9	5.05							
10	5.87							
11	6.91							
12	8.04							
13	0.101							
14	0.243							

We now select **Data Analysis**, and the list of tools available in the Toolpak is shown, as seen in the image below.

We select **Rank and Percentile**, and then specify our data range to analyse, which in this case is A2:A14, and we check the box that indicates a column label in our first row of data.

We want the output to start in column C, with the headings in row 2, with the output in rows 2 to 14 on the same worksheet.

You can see the choices in the image below.

	A2		▾		*fx*	Value		
	A	B	C	D	E	F	G	H
2	**Value**							
3	0.104							
4	0.247		Rank and Percentile				? ✕	
5	0.872		Input				OK	
6	1.47		Input Range:		$A$2:$A14	▦		
7	2.62		Grouped By:		⦿ Columns		Cancel	
8	3.96				○ Rows		Help	
9	5.05		☑ Labels in first row					
10	5.87		Output options					
11	6.91		⦿ Output Range:		$C$2:$C$14	▦		
12	8.04		○ New Worksheet Ply:					
13	0.101		○ New Workbook					
14	0.243							

Once we have entered our choices, the output is displayed in a table starting in column C as requested. This is shown in the image below in the highlighted section of the worksheet

	A	B	C	D	Formula Bar		G
2	**Value**		*Point*	*Value*	*Rank*	*Percent*	
3	0.104		10	8.04	1	100.00%	
4	0.247		9	6.91	2	90.90%	
5	0.872		8	5.87	3	81.80%	
6	1.47		7	5.05	4	72.70%	
7	2.62		6	3.96	5	63.60%	
8	3.96		5	2.62	6	54.50%	
9	5.05		4	1.47	7	45.40%	
10	5.87		3	0.872	8	36.30%	
11	6.91		2	0.247	9	27.20%	
12	8.04		12	0.243	10	18.10%	
13	0.101		1	0.104	11	9.00%	
14	0.243		11	0.101	12	0.00%	

As you can see, the original data is **Ranked** in descending order by value. The **Point** column gives the position of the data value in the original list, **Value** is the data value, **Rank** is its relative position in the ranking, 1 being the highest. The **Percent** column, shows what percentage of values are smaller than this value.

If the data set (list of values) includes duplicate values, these are given the same rank, as can be seen in rows 5, 6, 13 and 14 in the example below.

	A	B	C	D	E	F	G
2	**Value**		*Point*	*Value*	*Rank*	*Percent*	
3	0.104		10	8.04	1	100.00%	
4	0.247		9	6.91	2	90.90%	
5	0.872		7	5.87	3	72.70%	
6	1.47		8	5.87	3	72.70%	
7	2.62		6	3.96	5	63.60%	
8	3.96		5	2.62	6	54.50%	
9	5.87		4	1.47	7	45.40%	
10	5.87		3	0.872	8	36.30%	
11	6.91		2	0.247	9	27.20%	
12	8.04		12	0.243	10	18.10%	
13	0.104		1	0.104	11	0.00%	
14	0.243		11	0.104	11	0.00%	

If changes are made to the data values, the **Rank and Percentile** tool needs to be selected again, to update the analysis table.

moving averages

A moving average is a technique used to show trends in sets of data over a time period, for example the price of stocks and shares or sales figures. It is often used to 'smooth out' fluctuations and provide a more helpful trend line which can then be used to make a forecast of future values.

The **Moving Average** analysis tool calculates projected values over a given time period, based on the average value of the data over a specific number of preceding periods (the **interval**).

The **interval** is the number of data points used to calculate the moving average. The larger the interval, the smoother the moving average line; the smaller the interval, the more the moving average is affected by individual data point fluctuations.

For example, if we were looking at a 12 month period, the first value calculated might be the average for January, February, and March; the second would then be the average for February, March, and April; the third would be the average of March, April and May; and so on.

This tool can be useful to assist in the forecast of required stock levels, sales or similar time-based values, where you have figures over a reasonable period of time.

The example shown on the next page presents sales figures data which can be manipulated to create a **moving average** to project future sales levels.

◢	A	B	C	D	E	F	G	H
1	Sales forecast							
2								
3		January	February	March	April	May	June	July
4	Actual sales	£84,922	£85,780	£83,865	£93,670	£93,865	£96,040	
5								
6	Forecast sales							
7								

You can see from the above that we have actual sales figures for a six month period, which is not perhaps a very long time span in practice, but will be useful in helping to explain how a moving average can be produced and provide a guide for forecasting future sales.

The first step is to select **Data Analysis**, and then select the **Moving Average** tool:

◢	A	B	C	D	E	F	G	H
1	Sales forecast							
2								
3		January	February	March	April	May	June	July
4	Actual sales	£84,922	£85,780	£83,865	£93,670	£93,865	£96,040	
5								
6	Forecast sales							
7								

Data Analysis dialog box:

Analysis Tools
- Anova: Two-Factor With Replication
- Anova: Two-Factor Without Replication
- Correlation
- Covariance
- Descriptive Statistics
- Exponential Smoothing
- F-Test Two-Sample for Variances
- Fourier Analysis
- Histogram
- Moving Average

[OK] [Cancel] [Help]

We then select our **Input** range, to include all of our data, and the cell for July, for which we want a forecast value.

We leave the interval blank, which will cause the function to use the default of 3, hence calculating the moving average over 3 data points.

Similarly we define our **Output** range, where we want the calculated moving average values to be placed.

We can also select the **Chart Output** tick box to create a chart to give a visual impression of the values.

This selection process is illustrated in the screen image shown at the top of the next page.

When we have entered our choices, the moving average values are calculated and output in the specified range, as can be seen in the second image.

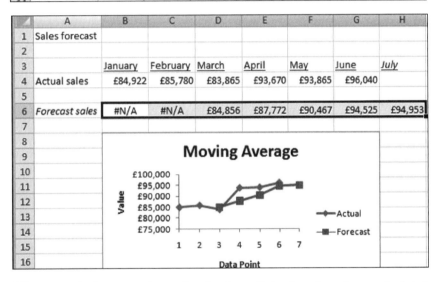

We can see in the screen immediately above that values have been calculated in Row 6 for March through to July (cell H6) which helps the business to forecast sales for July, ie a projected increase to £94,953.

Cells B6 and C6 contain N/A (Not Applicable), since they cannot be calculated. As we are using an interval of 3 (in this case months), these cells do not have enough data values preceding them to enable the software to carry out the moving average calculation.

An **important point to note** is that if you are using **Excel** software, the value produced by a three month moving average is recorded in the third (last) month, whereas in your accounting studies you may be used to seeing the average allocated to the second (middle) month. So if a 3 month moving average is calculated on the basis of the figures for January, February and March, Excel will record the figure in March rather than in February (as in the screen above).

histogram

When looking at a set of values, it is sometimes necessary to quantify how many values fall within certain categories, for example the ages of people in a class:

■ up to and including 16

■ between 17 and 30

■ between 31 and 60

and so on . . .

In histogram terms, these categories are known as **bins**. These are often shown as a series of rectangles, like a series of tower blocks of varying height, the area of which is equal to the **frequency** (the number) of the data items. In the example of the class, if it were a secondary school, there would be a far larger frequency and bin for the 'up to and including 16' age group whereas an adult class would have larger bins for the older age groups.

The **Histogram analysis** tool takes a list of data values (such as ages), and calculates how many of these values fall within the boundaries of each of the specified bins. This gives individual **frequencies** for the data bins from the set of data values.

In the image below we have some data values in column A, and we have defined our levels or bins, in columns C and D. We have defined 4 bins:

■ **Bin 1**   data values less than or equal to 25

■ **Bin 2**   data values greater than 25 and less than or equal to 50

■ **Bin 3**   data values greater than 50 and less than or equal to 75

■ **Bin 4**   data values greater than 75 and less than or equal to 100

Any values exceeding the final bin will be gathered under a bin of 'other'.

Bin values should be specified in ascending order.

	A	B	C	D	E	F	G	H
1	Values							
2	88		Bin 1	25				
3	74		Bin 2	50				
4	89		Bin 3	75				
5	65		Bin 4	100				
6	58							
7	47							
8	73							
9	68							
10	20							
11	65							

To achieve this in our spreadsheet we should select **Data Analysis**, and select the **Histogram** tool.

We select our **Input range**, to include all of our data in column A (this in fact includes 22 data values, the first 11 of which are shown above).

We select cells D2 to D5 as the range holding for our bin definitions (see screen image on previous page).

We define our **Output** range, where we want the frequency table to be placed.

We can also choose to create a **chart** of the frequency distribution of the data values.

This is done as follows:

Once we have entered our choices, the frequency values are calculated and output in the specified range, and the histogram chart created as can be seen in the image on the next page.

	A	B	C	D	E	F	G	H
2	88		Bin 1	25		Bin	Frequency	
3	74		Bin 2	50		25	3	
4	89		Bin 3	75		50	3	
5	65		Bin 4	100		75	10	
6	58					100	6	
7	47					More	0	
8	73							
9	68							
10	20							
11	65							
12	21							
13	27							
14	98							
15	11							
16	92							
17	82							
18	48							
19	57							

In the image above, you can see from the frequency table that

■ 3 of our values are less than or equal to 25

■ 3 are greater than 25 and less than or equal to 50

■ 10 are greater than 50 and less than or equal to 75

■ 6 are greater than 75 and less than or equal to 100

■ none ('more') is greater than 100

As you saw when you selected the above tools from the **Analysis Toolpak**, there are numerous other tools which will not be covered in this book. If time allows, you are recommended to experiment with and familiarise yourself with these other tools.

TYPES OF CHARTS

Within spreadsheet packages, there are a variety of different **chart** types available for the visual representation of data. In this section we are going to illustrate the following types of chart. Instructions for the creation of charts will follow in a separate section at the end of this chapter.

■ Bar

■ Line

■ Pie

■ Scatter

- Doughnut
- Bubble

bar chart

The bar chart is probably the most commonly used chart, and can be applied to data that is arranged in columns or rows on a worksheet.

In the image below, you can see that we have taken six months of sales data, and represented it as a **horizontal bar chart**, showing how the value of sales has changed over the period of six months. This is a bar chart in its simplest form, with only one set of data values. Note that bar charts can also be created with **vertical** bars; these are known as **column charts**.

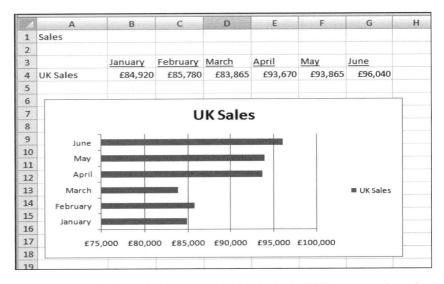

With two sets of data, sales in the UK and sales in the USA, we can show the values side by side, or stacked. The example below is side by side.

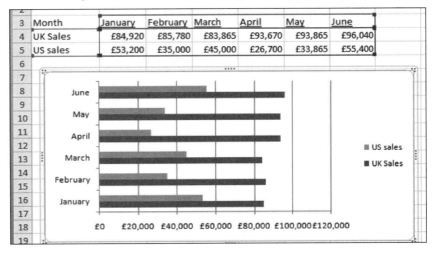

line chart

An example of a **line chart** using the same sales data is shown below. Line charts (or graphs) are ideal for showing trends in data over time and can be produced from data that is arranged in columns or rows on a worksheet.

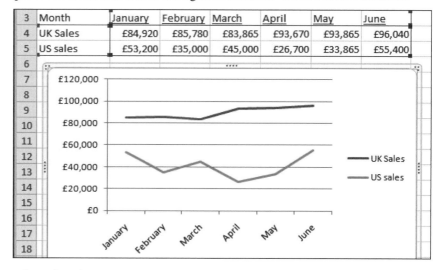

3	Month	January	February	March	April	May	June
4	UK Sales	£84,920	£85,780	£83,865	£93,670	£93,865	£96,040
5	US sales	£53,200	£35,000	£45,000	£26,700	£33,865	£55,400

pie chart

A **pie chart** can be produced for only one set of data values, arranged in one column or row on a worksheet. It is known as a 'pie chart' because it looks like a pie divided into a number of 'slices'.

To make the pie chart more visual, it is possible to select a **3D** chart and the slices will be shown as three dimensional, or **exploded** where the individual slices are separated. Both **3D** and **exploded** can also be selected at the same time. These options can add to a chart's clarity

Pie charts show the data values relative to the total of the values. Each data value is shown in a pie chart as a percentage or proportion of the whole 'pie'.

A pie chart can be used when:

- you only have one set of data values that you want to plot
- none of the values that you want to plot is negative
- very few of the values that you want to plot are zero
- you do not have more than seven values
- the data values represent all the parts of the whole

In the image on the next page you can see an example of a pie chart where the values represent the quantities of a certain product – eg a type of passenger plane – sold worldwide. These are set out in the Quantity Sold column for each country and are taken as the data values. Each value is then shown as a percentage of the whole on the pie chart.

	B	C	F	G	H	I	J	K
1	**Country**	**Quantity Sold**						
2	POL	150						
3	FR	200						
5	IT	85						
6	USA	235						
7	GER	124						
8	UK	375						
9								
10								
11								
12								
13								

Quantity Sold

- POL
- FR
- IT
- USA
- GER
- UK

13% 17% 7% 20% 11% 32%

scatter chart

A **scatter chart** can be produced for numeric data values that are arranged on a worksheet as adjacent rows or columns.

The two groups of numbers are plotted as one series of xy coordinates.

To use data on a worksheet for a scatter chart, you should have the x values in one row or column, and then the corresponding y values in the adjacent row or column.

Scatter charts are often used for displaying and comparing numeric values, such as scientific, statistical, and engineering data to show the relationships among several sets of numeric values.

An example of a scatter chart is shown in the image below, the data in columns A and B shows the price of coffee and the price of oil at the same points in time. This gives us a series of values which can be plotted as a scatter diagram. Each point on the diagram represents one pair of prices.

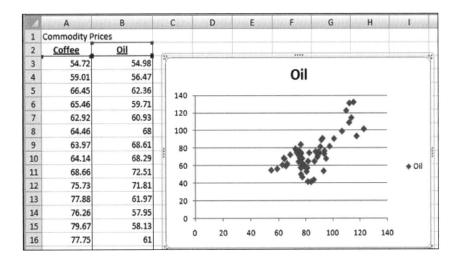

	A	B	C	D	E	F	G	H	I
1	Commodity Prices								
2	**Coffee**	**Oil**							
3	54.72	54.98							
4	59.01	56.47							
5	66.45	62.36							
6	65.46	59.71							
7	62.92	60.93							
8	64.46	68							
9	63.97	68.61							
10	64.14	68.29							
11	68.66	72.51							
12	75.73	71.81							
13	77.88	61.97							
14	76.26	57.95							
15	79.67	58.13							
16	77.75	61							

doughnut

A **doughnut chart** is similar to a pie chart, but can be produced for more than one set of data values, which are arranged in columns or rows on a worksheet. Whereas a pie is a solid circle cut into a slices, a doughnut often appears in the form of a series of concentric rings – ie rings grouped around the same centre.

Each ring of the doughnut represents a different data series, and each ring shows the data values relative to the total of the values for that series. This is seen clearly in the illustration below, which, like the pie chart, provides information about international sales.

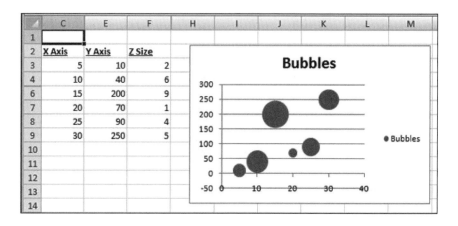

bubble

A **bubble chart** is a variation of a scatter chart in which the individual values are replaced with bubbles, and an additional dimension of the data is represented in the size of the bubbles. A bubble chart plots x values, y values, and z (size) values. You can see an example in the image below, where the three data series on the worksheet are represented on the bubble chart.

CREATING A CHART

We have seen that there are numerous chart types available to use. However the basic steps which can be used to create a chart from a worksheet are applicable to most chart types:

■ select the data on the worksheet to be presented in the chart

■ select the chart type required

■ enter a title and 'y' axis label for the chart

■ Label the 'x' axis to reflect the data shown (if applicable)

These steps are described and illustrated below, using sales data. This time the currency is Euros, and the sales are to Europe and Asia.

	A	B	C	D	E	F	G
1	Sales						
2							
3	Month	January	February	March	April	May	June
4	Europe	€ 84,920	€ 85,780	€ 83,865	€ 93,670	€ 93,865	€ 96,040
5	Asia	€ 53,200	€ 5,000	€ 45,000	€ 26,700	€ 33,865	€ 55,400
6							

Step 1 – select the data

Select the data, including the text which relates to the data. We are going to select both rows of data, since we want to compare the 2 rows of sales values. You could just select 1, if for example you wanted to create a pie chart.

	A	B	C	D	E	F	G
1	Sales						
2							
3	Month	January	February	March	April	May	June
4	Europe	€ 84,920	€ 85,780	€ 83,865	€ 93,670	€ 93,865	€ 96,040
5	Asia	€ 53,200	€ 5,000	€ 45,000	€ 26,700	€ 33,865	€ 55,400
6							

Note that in some versions of software, you may be taken through the chart creation by a 'help wizard', and may need to specify the range of your data. This can be done by either moving to the data and selecting as shown in the image above, or manually specify the range, in this case $A$3:$G$5, always using absolute cell addresses.

Step 2 – select the chart type

Select **Insert chart** from the menu and then the type of chart required. In this example we are going to create a line chart to represent both rows of data.

A chart is created on the same worksheet by default.

This chart can be moved around the worksheet by selecting it with mouse, or it can be moved to another worksheet, using the **Move chart** option. It can also be resized, by selecting and moving at the corners.

In the image below, we have created a line chart, and placed it below our rows of data.

Step 3 – give the chart a title and the y-axis a label

The chart axes are automatically created with scales based on the ranges of values in the data. The key (**legend**), which identifies which line on the graph represents which series of data, is shown to the right by default.

To introduce a title for the **chart** and a **label** for the y axis (the vertical axis), select the chart itself with a single or double click, and you can then select a different **Chart layout** from the **Chart design menu** which includes a chart title and a label for the y axis.

In the image at the top of the next page, you can see that **default titles** for the Chart and the 'y' axis appear. It is very simple to change this text, by selecting the individual title and entering the required text. Here it is 'Sales value'. The completed version of the chart, with title and label amended, is shown in the second image on the next page.

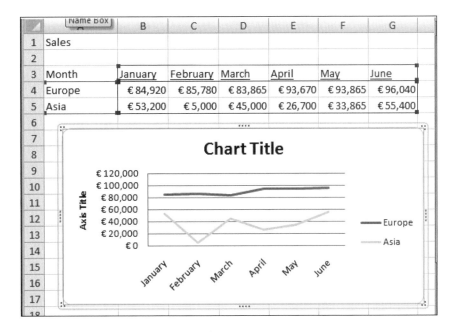

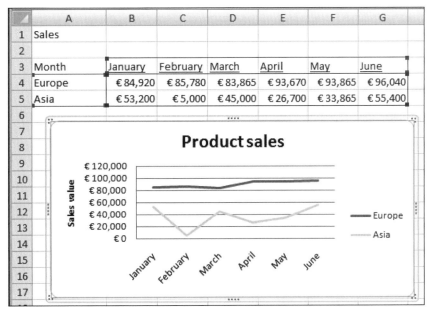

Step 4 – dealing with the 'x' axis

The layout we have used does not include an axis label for the x axis. To add this manually:

■ Select the chart (single or double click)

■ From the **Chart menu**, select the **Layout** tab

■ Select **Axis Titles**, **Primary Horizontal Axis** title

■ At present this will show none, so select **Title below Axis**

■ Edit the 'x' axis label as required – here 'Month' is the chosen axis title

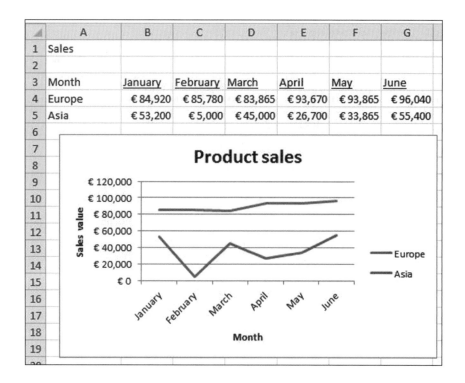

Step 5 – changing one of the graph types

Once we have created our chart representing 2 sets of data, it is possible to change how one of the sets of data is shown on the chart. For example, we may want to show the data from Asia as a bar chart, still keeping the European sales as a line graph.

To do this:

■ right mouse click on the line representing the Asia data on the chart (each data point will be highlighted)

■ select **Change Series Chart Type**

■ select **Column** and OK

The chart should now look as shown in the image on the next page.

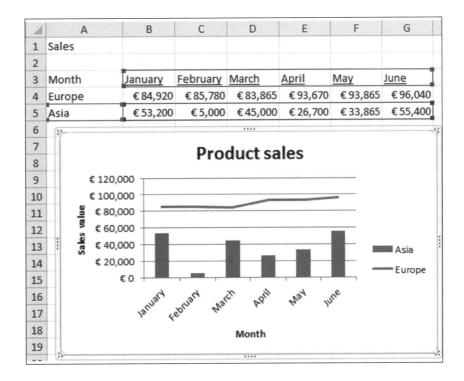

Step 6 – moving or re-sizing

Once you have created a chart as described in the previous steps, you may wish to move the chart to a different location either on the same or a different worksheet, for example to avoid it covering some of the data.

To do this:

- click on the outermost frame of the chart (you will see the cursor changes to a black cross with arrow heads)

- hold down the left mouse key and drag the chart to its new position

If you want to **move** the chart to a new worksheet:

- click with the right mouse within the space surrounding the chart, but still within the chart frame

- select **Move chart** from the menu

- select the sheet the chart is to move to

It is also possible that you might want to change the size of the chart.

To **resize** a chart:

- click on the chart to select it

- place the cursor over one of the corners of the chart frame, or the dots around the edges of the frame (you will see the cursor changes to a double headed arrow)

- hold down the left mouse key and drag to the required size.

scatter chart with trend line

One of the charts previously mentioned is the **scatter chart**. It is very simple to introduce a **trend line** onto the scatter chart.

To create a trend line on a scatter chart:

- select the scatter chart (double click)

- from the **Chart menu**, select the **Layout** tab

- select **Trendline** from the menu

- change from **None** to the required type of trendline

charts – learning about the software

As you will see from reading this chapter and also experimenting with the spreadsheet software, there are many things which can be changed within the chart layout itself, such as:

- the position of the legend

- displaying gridlines

- how the scales are to be shown

- how data points are to be shown on the lines

As you will see, not all these areas are covered in this text, but you are strongly recommended to experiment with your own data. Spreadsheet software is an essentially practical 'hands on ' subject.

As previously mentioned, different software packages will step through the chart creation process in different ways, so it is important to familiarise yourself with the processes involved.

Chapter Summary

Our discussion of charts concludes the text of this chapter, which has covered:

■ simple statistical functions

■ analysis tools

■ types of charts

■ creating charts

You should now carry out some or all of the exercises on the next few pages in order to practise and reinforce your learning.

Activities

Exercise 1 – displaying car sales figures

In this first exercise we will open an existing spreadsheet containing some data, add some further data, to practise using the simple statistical functions and producing some charts.

To obtain this spreadsheet visit www.osbornebooks.co.uk ('Resources') and download filename **T6cars**.

Stage 1

This stage is about starting to introduce some simple statistical formulas into our spreadsheet which records monthly car sales for various manufacturers.

1. Download the workbook **T6cars**

2. Open the downloaded file, save the workbook with new name **T6Exercise1**

   The workbook should appear as shown below.

	A	B	C	D	E	F	G	H
1	Car Sales							
2		Jan	Feb	Mar	Apr	May	Jun	
3	Ford	25090	25000	60000	25010	30900	24000	
4	Volkswagen	13200	6150	32900	15130	15040	16090	
5	Hyundai	1000	1500	2500	1000	1000	2000	
6	Skoda	1200	2800	4000	3500	2130	1770	
7	Renault	7000	32090	25600	9230	9100	11800	
8	Vauxhall	22000	10500	55000	25050	24100	30100	

3. Insert a row between rows 1 and 2.

4. Insert the following additional row between Skoda, and Renault (rows 6 and 7).

	Jan	Feb	Mar	Apr	May	Jun
Kia	930	1050	5430	1500	2110	2340

5. Merge cells H2, and I2 enter the text *Average*, in bold and italics aligned in the centre.

6. In cell H3, enter *3 month* in bold and italics.

7.   In cell I3 enter *6 month* in bold and italics.

8.   Format the cells in row 3, so that the text is aligned to the right of the cells, and the font style is bold and italics.

9.   In cell H4, enter a formula to calculate the Average for February, April and June.

10. Copy this formula to cells H5 through to H10.

11. In cell I4, enter a formula to calculate the average over all 6 months.

12. Copy this formula to cells I5 through to I10.

13. Format all numeric cells to include a comma (,) to represent thousands, and no decimal places.

14. Save the workbook with the same name **T6Exercise1**

     Your spreadsheet should now look as shown in the image below.

	A	B	C	D	E	F	G	H	I
1	Car Sales								
2								*Average*	
3		*Jan*	*Feb*	*Mar*	*Apr*	*May*	*Jun*	*3 month*	*6 month*
4	Ford	25,090	25,000	60,000	25,010	30,900	24,000	24,670	31,667
5	Volkswagen	13,200	6,150	32,900	15,130	15,040	16,090	12,457	16,418
6	Hyundai	1,000	1,500	2,500	1,000	1,000	2,000	1,500	1,500
7	Skoda	1,200	2,800	4,000	3,500	2,130	1,770	2,690	2,567
8	Kia	930	1,050	5,430	1,500	2,110	2,340	1,630	2,227
9	Renault	7,000	32,090	25,600	9,230	9,100	11,800	17,707	15,803
10	Vauxhall	22,000	10,500	55,000	25,050	24,100	30,100	21,883	27,792
11									

The image below shows the formulas behind the calculations

	A	B	C	D	E	F	G	H	I
1	Car Sales								
2								*Average*	
3		*Jan*	*Feb*	*Mar*	*Apr*	*May*	*Jun*	*3 month*	*6 month*
4	Ford	25090	25000	60000	25010	30900	24000	=AVERAGE(C4,E4,G4)	=AVERAGE(B4:G4)
5	Volkswagen	13200	6150	32900	15130	15040	16090	=AVERAGE(C5,E5,G5)	=AVERAGE(B5:G5)
6	Hyundai	1000	1500	2500	1000	1000	2000	=AVERAGE(C6,E6,G6)	=AVERAGE(B6:G6)
7	Skoda	1200	2800	4000	3500	2130	1770	=AVERAGE(C7,E7,G7)	=AVERAGE(B7:G7)
8	Kia	930	1050	5430	1500	2110	2340	=AVERAGE(C8,E8,G8)	=AVERAGE(B8:G8)
9	Renault	7000	32090	25600	9230	9100	11800	=AVERAGE(C9,E9,G9)	=AVERAGE(B9:G9)
10	Vauxhall	22000	10500	55000	25050	24100	30100	=AVERAGE(C10,E10,G10)	=AVERAGE(B10:G10)

Stage 2

In this stage we are going to include further calculations to the car sales spreadsheet.

1.   Insert 2 rows between rows 1 and 2.

2.   In cell A3, enter the text *Max*, in bold and italics, aligned right.

3.   In cell B3, enter a formula to calculate the maximum figure from all the monthly values, using the MAX function.

4.   In cell C3, enter the text *Min*, in bold and italics, aligned right.

5.   In cell D3, enter a formula to calculate the minimum figure from all the monthly values, using the MIN function.

6.   In cell E3, enter the text *Count*, in bold and italics, aligned right.

7.   In cell F3, enter a formula to calculate how many numeric monthly values there are in the data in columns B to G, rows 6 to 12, using the COUNT function.

8.   Underline the values in cells B3, D3 and F3

9.   Save your spreadsheet (keeping the same name – **T6Exercise1**)

        Your spreadsheet should now appear as shown below.

	A	B	C	D	E	F	G	H	I
1	Car Sales								
2									
3	*Max*	60,000	*Min*	930	*Count*	42			
4								Average	
5		Jan	Feb	Mar	Apr	May	Jun	3 month	6 month
6	Ford	25,090	25,000	60,000	25,010	30,900	24,000	24,670	31,667
7	Volkswagen	13,200	6,150	32,900	15,130	15,040	16,090	12,457	16,418
8	Hyundai	1,000	1,500	2,500	1,000	1,000	2,000	1,500	1,500
9	Skoda	1,200	2,800	4,000	3,500	2,130	1,770	2,690	2,567
10	Kia	930	1,050	5,430	1,500	2,110	2,340	1,630	2,227
11	Renault	7,000	32,090	25,600	9,230	9,100	11,800	17,707	15,803
12	Vauxhall	22,000	10,500	55,000	25,050	24,100	30,100	21,883	27,792

Stage 3

We are now going to create a line chart, to compare Ford sales with those of Volkswagen.

1.   Select the cells A5 through to G7, this includes the column headings, row headings and data for the 6 months for Ford and Volkswagen.

2.   Insert a **line chart** to represent this data.

3.   Move the chart to below the data.

4.   Using the chart **Design** options, choose a display which gives the chart a title and a label for the y axis. (usually layout1), or using **Chart Layout**, **Chart Title** and **Axis Titles**.

5.   Change the chart title to be **Car Sales January to June**

6.   Change the y axis title to be **No. of cars**

7.   Add a title for the x axis, and change it to read **Month**.

8.   Select and extend/stretch the graph so that it is a similar width to the data above it.

9.   Save your spreadsheet (keeping the same name – **T6Exercise1**)

Your spreadsheet should now look as shown below.

	A	B	C	D	E	F	G	H	I
1	Car Sales								
2									
3	*Max*	60,000	*Min*	930	*Count*	42			
4								*Average*	
5		*Jan*	*Feb*	*Mar*	*Apr*	*May*	*Jun*	*3 month*	*6 month*
6	Ford	25,090	25,000	60,000	25,010	30,900	24,000	24,670	31,667
7	Volkswagen	13,200	6,150	32,900	15,130	15,040	16,090	12,457	16,418
8	Hyundai	1,000	1,500	2,500	1,000	1,000	2,000	1,500	1,500
9	Skoda	1,200	2,800	4,000	3,500	2,130	1,770	2,690	2,567
10	Kia	930	1,050	5,430	1,500	2,110	2,340	1,630	2,227
11	Renault	7,000	32,090	25,600	9,230	9,100	11,800	17,707	15,803
12	Vauxhall	22,000	10,500	55,000	25,050	24,100	30,100	21,883	27,792
13									

Car Sales January to June line chart with y-axis labelled "No. of Cars" (0 to 80,000), x-axis labelled "Month" (Jan to Jun), showing Ford and Volkswagen series.

Stage 4

We are now going to create a pie chart to provide an indicator of the market share of each car manufacturer based on recorded sales.

1.   Remove the existing line chart.

2.   Move the four cells A3, B3, C3, D3 one cell to the right, so that Max is in cell B3, and so on.

3.   Insert a column between columns A and B.

4.   In cell B5 enter the text **Totals**, in bold.

5.   In cell B6, enter a formula to calculate the total sales over the 6 month period (January through to June).

6.   Copy the formula into cells B7 through to B12.

7.   Select the cells A5 through to B12, this includes the column headings, row headings and totals data for Ford to Vauxhall.

8.   Insert a pie chart to represent this data.

9.   Move the chart to below the data.

10.   We need to modify this default layout to include the percentage values. Select the pie chart, right click and select **Add Data Labels**. The numeric values representing each portion will appear. Now select the chart again, right click and select **Format Data Labels**. Check the appropriate boxes for the values to display as percentages rather than values.

11.   Change the chart title from **Totals** to **6 months totals**.

12.   Save your spreadsheet (keeping the same name – **T6Exercise1**)

       Your spreadsheet should now look as shown on the next page.

       Note that the different coloured portions of the pie chart which appear in different colours on the screen show as different shades of grey in this text.

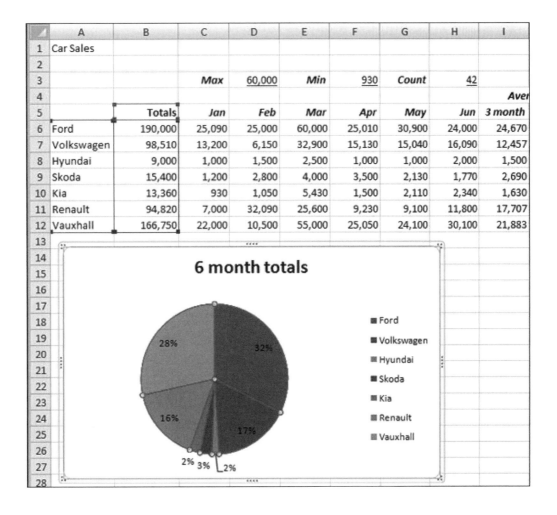

	A	B	C	D	E	F	G	H	I
1	Car Sales								
2									
3			*Max*	60,000	*Min*	930	*Count*	42	
4									*Aver*
5		*Totals*	*Jan*	*Feb*	*Mar*	*Apr*	*May*	*Jun*	*3 month*
6	Ford	190,000	25,090	25,000	60,000	25,010	30,900	24,000	24,670
7	Volkswagen	98,510	13,200	6,150	32,900	15,130	15,040	16,090	12,457
8	Hyundai	9,000	1,000	1,500	2,500	1,000	1,000	2,000	1,500
9	Skoda	15,400	1,200	2,800	4,000	3,500	2,130	1,770	2,690
10	Kia	13,360	930	1,050	5,430	1,500	2,110	2,340	1,630
11	Renault	94,820	7,000	32,090	25,600	9,230	9,100	11,800	17,707
12	Vauxhall	166,750	22,000	10,500	55,000	25,050	24,100	30,100	21,883

6 month totals

- Ford 32%
- Volkswagen 28%
- Hyundai 16%
- Skoda 17%
- Kia 2%
- Renault 3%
- Vauxhall 2%

Exercise 2 – using the analysis toolpak

In this next exercise we are going to use the tools found in the **Analysis Toolpak** (Excel only). We are again going to make use of an existing spreadsheet.

To obtain this spreadsheet visit www.osbornebooks.co.uk ('Resources') and download filename **T6toolpak**

Stage 1

This stage will get us started with the **Analysis Toolpak**, and then we are going to make use of some data previously created, within the file **T6toolpak** to create a **Rank and Percentile** table from a list of values

1.   The first step is to check that the **Analysis Toolpak** is available in your spreadsheet software, as described previously in this chapter. If it is not available, you may be able to install it yourself, guided by the instructions, provided. Alternatively you may not have the necessary authority, and may need to refer to your technical support.

2.   Download the workbook **T6toolpak**

3.   Open the downloaded file, Save the workbook with the name **T6Exercise2**

      The workbook should look as shown below.

	A	B	C	D	E	
1	Values					
2	88					
3	74					
4	89					
5	65					
6	58					
7	47					
8	73					
9	68					
10	20					
11	65					
12	21					
13	27					
14	98					
15	11					
16	92					

4.   Select **Data Analysis** from the Data or Tools menu, select **Rank and Percentile**.

5.   Either enter the **input range** of data A2 to A16 using absolute cell references, or select the range using the mouse.

6.   Since the data is all in column A, **Grouped by** should be **Columns**.

7. Select **Output range** (rather than new worksheet), enter or select cell D1, (absolute reference $D$1), so that the table will start output in cell D1.

8. The **Rank and Percentile** table will be displayed.

9. Save your spreadsheet (keeping the same name - **T6Exercise2**).

Your spreadsheet should now appear as shown below.

	A	B	C	D	E	F	G
1	Values			Point	Column1	Rank	Percent
2	88			13	98	1	100.00%
3	74			15	92	2	92.80%
4	89			3	89	3	85.70%
5	65			1	88	4	78.50%
6	58			2	74	5	71.40%
7	47			7	73	6	64.20%
8	73			8	68	7	57.10%
9	68			4	65	8	42.80%
10	20			10	65	8	42.80%
11	65			5	58	10	35.70%
12	21			6	47	11	28.50%
13	27			12	27	12	21.40%
14	98			11	21	13	14.20%
15	11			9	20	14	7.10%
16	92			14	11	15	0.00%

Stage 2

We are now going to make use of the same data to create a histogram, to analyse the frequency of different numbers in our data. To do this we are going to copy the values column in column A to another worksheet in the workbook.

1. Check that you have a second worksheet in the workbook you have open, if not, add a worksheet (as described in Chapter 1) and name it **histogram**.

2. Select column A (the values column) on worksheet **sheet1**, using Copy and Paste, copy this information to column A on worksheet **histogram**.

3. Select worksheet **histogram**.

We now need to define how we want to split the data up in order to analyse it, We do this by using the **bins** we referred to in the chapter. In this instance we are going to have 3 bins:

■ for numbers less than or equal to 30

■ for numbers greater than 30 and less than or equal to 60

■ for numbers greater than 60 and less than or equal to 90

4. In cell C2, enter the text **Bin 1**, and in cell D2 enter **30**.

5. In cell C3, enter the text **Bin 2**, and cell D3 enter **60**.

6. In cell C4, enter the text **Bin 3**, and cell D4 enter **90**.

7. Select **Data Analysis** from the Data or Tools menu, and then select **Histogram**.

8. Either enter the **Input range** of data A2 to A16 using absolute cell references, or select the range using the mouse.

9. Either enter the **Bin range** of data D2 to D4 using absolute cell references, or select the range using the mouse.

10. Select **Output range** (rather than new worksheet), enter or select cell F2, so that the table will start output in cell F2.

11. Select **Chart Output**.

12. The histogram frequency table and the chart will be displayed.

13. Select and move the chart to be positioned under the bins and frequency tables.

14. Save your spreadsheet (keeping the same name - **T6Exercise2**).

Your spreadsheet should now look as shown on the next page.

	A	B	C	D	E	F	G	H
1	Values							
2	88		Bin 1	30		*Bin*	*Frequency*	
3	74		Bin 2	60		30	4	
4	89		Bin 3	90		60	2	
5	65					90	7	
6	58					More	2	
7	47							
8	73							
9	68							
10	20							
11	65							
12	21							
13	27							
14	98							
15	11							
16	92							
17								

Stage 3

We are going to enter some data values which we will then use to create an additional forecast value for July using the moving average tool.

1. Check that you have a third worksheet in the workbook you have open, if not add a worksheet (as described in Chapter 1) and name it **average**.

2. Select worksheet **average**, enter **Car Sales** in cell A1.

3. Enter the values in the table below, with Jan in cell B3, aligning all the month names to the right.

	Jan	Feb	Mar	Apr	May	Jun	July
Ford	25090	25000	60000	25010	30900	24000	

4. In cell A5 enter **Forecast**.

5. Select **Data Analysis** from the Data or Tools menu, select **Moving average**.

6. Either enter the **Input range** of data B4 to H4 using absolute cell references, or select the range using the mouse.

7. Leave **Labels in first** row unchecked.

8.   Enter 3 in **Interval** (the normal default)

9.   Select **Output** range, enter B5 to H5 using absolute cell references, or select the range using the mouse.

10.   Select **Chart output**.

11.   The **moving average values** will be created in row 5, showing a forecast value for July, and the moving average chart will be displayed, comparing the actual values against the forecast.

12.   If necessary, move the chart to be positioned under data.

13.   Save your spreadsheet (keeping the same name - **T6Exercise2**).

Your spreadsheet should now appear as shown below. Note that the first average figure is recorded in the third month (Mar) rather than in the second (Feb), as explained on page 153.

	A	B	C	D	E	F	G	H
1	Car Sales							
2								
3		Jan	Feb	Mar	Apr	May	Jun	July
4	Ford	25090	25000	60000	25010	30900	24000	
5	Forecast	#N/A	#N/A	36696.67	36670	38636.67	26636.67	27450
6								
7								
8								
9								
10								
11								
12								
13								
14								
15								
16								

You have now completed the second exercise.

Exercise 3 – creating charts

In this next exercise we are going to practise creating three other types of chart:

•   bar

•   scatter

•   doughnut

For some of the charts we will download the data, and for others we will enter a small amount of data.

To access and download the necessary workbooks, visit www.osbornebooks.co.uk ('Resources').

Stage 1

In this stage we will create a bar chart with a previously created workbook in order to compare the sales of the two car manufacturers over a six month period.

1.   Open a new workbook.

2.   Enter the data shown in the table below, again relating to car sales.

Car sales						
	Jan	**Feb**	**Mar**	**Apr**	**May**	**Jun**
Hyundai	1000	1500	2500	1000	1000	2000
Skoda	1200	2800	4000	3500	2130	1770

3.   Save the workbook with new name **T6Exercise3**.

4.   Select the cells A2 through to G4, this includes the column headings, row headings and data for the 6 months for Hyundai and Skoda.

5.   Insert a **Bar Chart** (if given a choice of styles, select 2D) to represent this data.

6.   Move the chart and resize to the same width as the data, and positioned below the data.

7.   Using chart **Layout**, **Chart Title** and **Axis Titles** add titles to the chart layout.

8.   Change the chart title to be **Car sales January to June**

9.   Change the y axis title to be **Months**.

10.   Add a title for the x axis, and change it to read **Qty sold**.

11. Save your spreadsheet (keeping the same name – **T6Exercise3**)

Your spreadsheet should now appear as shown below:

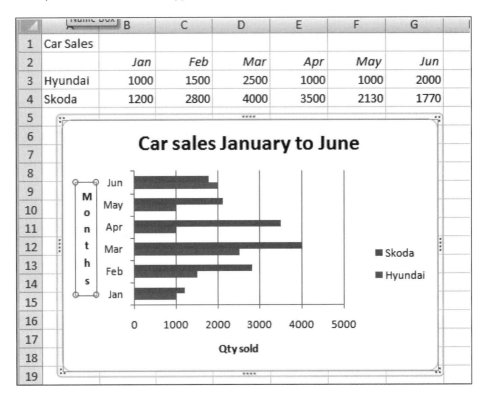

Stage 2

We are now going to use this same data to create a **doughnut** chart.

1. Check that you have a second worksheet in the workbook you have open, if not add a worksheet (as described in Chapter 1) and name it **doughnut**.

2. Select all the data on your original worksheet (excluding the chart), using Copy and Paste, copy this information to column A on worksheet **doughnut**.

3. Select worksheet **doughnut**.

4. Select the cells A2 through to G4; this includes the column headings, row headings and data for the 6 months for Hyundai and Skoda.

5. Insert a **doughnut chart** to represent this data.

6. Move the chart and resize to the same width as the data, and position below the data.

7. Using chart **Layout**, **Chart Title** add a title to the chart layout.

8. Change the chart title to be **Hyundai and Skoda**.

9. For each ring of the doughnut chart, select **Add Data Labels** (from the drop-down menu shown by a right mouse click on the doughnut ring), so that the value of each segment is displayed.

10. For each ring of the doughnut chart, now select **Format Data Labels** (from the drop-down menu shown by a right mouse click on the doughnut ring), so that the label that includes the **Series Name**, is displayed as a **percentage**, rather than a value, and has (**New Line**) selected as the **Separator**.

11. Save your spreadsheet (keeping the same name – **T6Exercise3**)

Your spreadsheet should now appear as shown below.

	A	B	C	D	E	F	G	H
1	Car Sales							
2		Jan	Feb	Mar	Apr	May	Jun	
3	Hyundai	1000	1500	2500	1000	1000	2000	
4	Skoda	1200	2800	4000	3500	2130	1770	

Stage 3

We are now going to use some financial data to create a scatter chart from a series of twelve values held in a previously created workbook. The data represents the values of two stock market indices which chart the value of the UK and US stock markets at different points in time. The stock market indices involved are the FTSE (UK stocks and shares) and the Dow (US stock and shares).

1. Download the workbook **T6scatter** from www.osbornebooks.co.uk ('Resources').

2. Open the downloaded file, save the workbook with new name **T6Exercise33**.

    The workbook screen should appear as shown below. You should appreciate that there will be more values off to the right, which are not shown in this image.

	A	B	C	D	E	F	G	H	I
	A9				*fx*				
1	Financial data								
2									
3	FTSE	5,322	5,534	5,060	5,599	5,770	5,123	5,126	5,132
4	DOW	10,388	10,618	10,012	10,566	10,997	10,380	9,931	10,198
5									
6									

Sheet1 / Sheet2 / Sheet3

3. Select all the data on the worksheet, cells A3 through to M4.

4. Insert a **scatter chart** to represent this data.

5. Move the chart to a position below and to the left of the data.

6. Using chart **Layout**, **Trendline** add a linear trendline to the chart.

7. Use **Layout, Axis Titles** to add titles to the axis.

8. Save your spreadsheet (keeping the same name – **T6Exercise33**)

Your spreadsheet should now appear as shown on the next page.

	A	B	C	D	E	F	G	H	I
1	Financial data								
2									
3	FTSE	5,322	5,534	5,060	5,599	5,770	5,123	5,126	5,132
4	DOW	10,388	10,618	10,012	10,566	10,997	10,380	9,931	10,198
5									

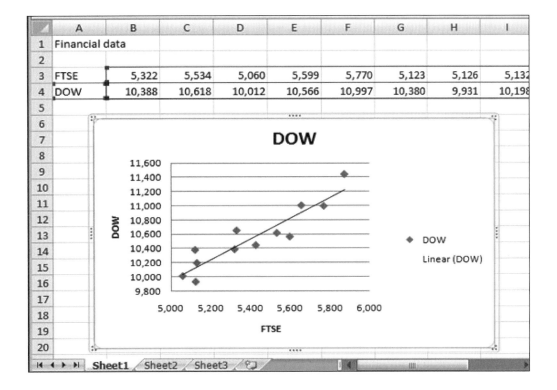

7 Pivot tables and workbook management

this chapter covers...

This chapter covers some further spreadsheet techniques such as window management using Freeze Panes. It also explains the use of pivot tables and describes how they are created and formatted. By the time you have finished this chapter and carried out the exercises which follow, you should be able to produce spreadsheets which are very comprehensive, easy to read and containing pivot tables.

The concepts and techniques covered are:

- *managing windows – using freeze panes*

- *using the Paste Special function*

- *working with multiple worksheets and workbooks*

- *the reasons for using a pivot table*

- *creating a simple pivot table*

- *using subsets of data*

- *formatting pivot tables*

- *what-if scenarios*

- *goal seeking*

- *data tables*

Note that the the step-by-step instructions given in this chapter are based on the Microsoft ® Excel model, but the concepts and techniques described generally relate to all spreadsheet packages.

WINDOW – FREEZE PANES

As we have seen in earlier chapters, we can scroll up, down and across our worksheet using the scroll bars positioned around the working area of the worksheet.

However, sometimes if we have a large amount of data, we want still to be able to see our row or column text headings so that we know what data we are looking at. The problem is illustrated in the next two screen images.

If we look at the image below, we can see the top portion of a large spreadsheet recording customer sales. The headings are clearly visible.

	A	B	C	D	E	F	G	H	I
1	Name	Total	Month1	Month2	Month3	Month4	Month5	Month6	Month7
2	Farmhouse Foods	£154	£0	£112	£0	£0	£0	£26	£0
3	Engineering Services	£554	£0	£0	£0	£0	£67	£0	£0
4	Another Food Service	£790	£0	£0	£0	£58	£116	£0	£0
5	Top Quality Supplies	£56	£0	£56	£0	£0	£0	£0	£0
6	Halal Foods	£36	£0	£0	£0	£0	£0	£0	£0
7	Edwards Farm	£195	£0	£0	£0	£0	£40	£0	£65
8	Allen and co	£1,412	£45	£68	£231	£0	£331	£37	£49
9	Ahmed and son	£340	£0	£0	£0	£0	£0	£0	£0
10	Green & Sons Wholesalers	£1,827	£700	£0	£104	£0	£0	£0	£0
11	Higginbottom and son	£389	£0	£0	£0	£0	£0	£0	£300
12	W B Meats	£135	£0	£45	£0	£0	£0	£0	£0

If we use the scroll bars to move around the data, we can end up in a situation where we cannot see the text at the top of the column, or at the start of the row. This is not very useful, as you can see in the image shown below.

	C	D	E	F	G	H	I	J	K	L	M
4	£0	£0	£0	£58	£116	£0	£0	£174	£0	£0	£0
5	£0	£56	£0	£0	£0	£0	£0	£0	£0	£0	£0
6	£0	£0	£0	£0	£0	£0	£0	£0	£0	£0	£36
7	£0	£0	£0	£0	£40	£0	£65	£0	£0	£0	£0
8	£45	£68	£231	£0	£331	£37	£49	£0	£0	£100	£115
9	£0	£0	£0	£0	£0	£0	£0	£0	£0	£0	£0
10	£700	£0	£104	£0	£0	£0	£0	£0	£363	£0	£0
11	£0	£0	£0	£0	£0	£0	£300	£0	£0	£0	£89
12	£0	£45	£0	£0	£0	£0	£0	£0	£0	£0	£0
13	£0	£0	£50	£0	£0	£0	£0	£25	£0	£0	£0
14	£458	£166	£583	£225	£414	£365	£470	£490	£244	£423	£354
15	£0	£40	£0	£0	£0	£0	£0	£0	£0	£0	£0

H ◄ ► H   Customer Sales   Sheet2   Sheet3

To get over this problem we can use a facility called **Freeze Panes**. This facility is found under the **View** menu if you are using Excel.

There are several choices within **Freeze Panes**, but the simplest is to select the first data cell (B2 in our example), then select **Freeze Panes** from the appropriate menu.

You are now able to scroll up and down with row and column headings staying in view, as can be seen in the image below, where we have scrolled both right and down. The solid black lines at the bottom of row1 and to the right of column A indicate they are frozen and will not disappear out of view as you scroll around the worksheet.

	A	G	H	I	J	K	L	M	N
1	**Name**	**Month5**	**Month6**	**Month7**	**Month8**	**Month9**	**Mont10**	**Month11**	**Month12**
13	The Halal Centre	£0	£0	£0	£25	£0	£0	£0	£0
14	T F Curries	£414	£365	£470	£490	£244	£423	£354	£560
15	Fiber Optical Services	£0	£0	£0	£0	£0	£0	£0	£0
16	My Provisions	£0	£0	£0	£25	£0	£0	£0	£0
17	Alliance services	£0	£0	£0	£0	£0	£0	£0	£0
18	Aluminium casts	£360	£119	£72	£286	£0	£2,093	£0	£364
19	Impala	£0	£98	£0	£0	£0	£0	£0	£0
20	Tool Hire	£0	£0	£0	£0	£0	£0	£0	£0
21	Handyfreight	£0	£0	£0	£0	£0	£0	£0	£0
22	Steel Traders	£0	£0	£0	£0	£0	£0	£0	£0
23	Fruit Supplies	£0	£0	£0	£0	£65	£0	£279	£0

Customer Sales / Sheet2 / Sheet3 / ?

PASTE SPECIAL

This is an extremely useful facility when we are copying data, whether it be a formula or just some text in a cell or group of cells.

Paste Special allows us to decide exactly how we want to paste this copied information into its new location.

For example, if it is some text we are copying, formatted in **Bold** and **Underlined**, we may not want the copied text to be formatted in the same way. Or perhaps, we have a formula which we are copying, and we don't want to copy the formula, but the actual value it produces instead to paste in to the new location.

Looking at the image below, we have selected four cells of text, A6 to D6.

	A	B	C	D	E
1	Bank transactions				
2					
3	Opening balance	1,500.00			
4	Closing balance	1,289.05			**Down
5					
6	Date	Debit	Credit	Balance	
7	02/07/2010	95.34	0.00	1,404.66	

Once you have selected the data which you want to copy (cells A6:D6 as shown on the previous page) select **Copy**, move to where you want to place the copy – in this case, cell A14 – and select **Paste Special** from the menu. The **Paste Special** options appear as shown below.

In this case we just want to copy the values, without formats, so we select **Values**, and OK. The results are shown in the screen image below, with the copy of the unformatted text shown in cells A14:D14.

By choosing the **Values** button you will paste the values resulting from formulas (rather than the formulas themselves) without formatting. If you wish to paste the actual formulas without formatting then the **Formulas** button should be chosen

	A	B	C	D	E	F
1	Bank transactions					
2						
3	Opening balance	1,500.00				
4	Closing balance	1,289.05			**Down	
5						
6	Date	Debit	Credit	Balance		
7	02/07/2010	95.34	0.00	1,404.66		
8	11/07/2010	0.00	25.50	1,430.16		
9	15/07/2010	0.00	34.78	1,464.94		
10	22/07/2010	67.90	0.00	1,397.04		
11	28/07/2010	107.99	0.00	1,289.05		
12	Totals	271.23	60.28		1,289.05	
13						
14	Date	Debit	Credit	Balance		

WORKING WITH MULTIPLE WORKSHEETS

When creating a formula, it is possible to use or reference data **on another worksheet** within the same workbook by including the worksheet name within the formula.

If we look at the images below, we can see a simple workbook with two worksheets, one named **July**, the other named **Adjust**.

The July worksheet shows the opening and closing bank balances for the month:

The Adjust worksheet (shown below) is very simple, containing adjustment figures which need to be incorporated in the monthly bank balance.

In this case we want cell B5 on worksheet July, to contain the adjustment value for July, found in cell D3 on worksheet Adjust. To do this:-

■   Move to cell B5 on worksheet July

■   Enter **=** (to indicate a formula)

■   Move to cell D3 on worksheet Adjust

■   Press **RETURN** to complete the formula

Looking at the image below we can see the formula created in cell B5 in the formula bar of worksheet July:

=Adjust!D3

The formula contains a direct reference to the work sheet **Adjust**, followed by an exclamation mark (!) to indicate that this is a worksheet name, and then the cell reference D3 in the worksheet Adjust.

copying a worksheet

It is very simple to make a copy of a worksheet:

■ select the worksheet you want to copy

■ right mouse click on the worksheet name tab

■ select **Move** or **Copy**

This operation can be seen below in the screen image below.

- choose where the copy sheet is to be placed in the workbook,

- select the **Create a copy** check box, so that it is ticked.

- press OK

The screen will appear as follows:

In the example shown above a copy of the worksheet will be placed at the end of the workbook.

WORKING WITH MULTIPLE WORKBOOKS

In the last section we described working within more than one worksheet.

It is also possible to move or copy a worksheet from one workbook to another workbook. The procedure is very similar to moving worksheets within a single workbook. To move or copy a worksheet from one workbook to another workbook:

- in the **To book** box, select the name of the workbook where the worksheet is to be moved or copied to (in the example which follows we select **new book** from the drop down list)

- choose in which workbook the copy worksheet is to be placed

- select the **Create a copy** check box, so that it is ticked, and press OK

The screen will appear as shown at the top of the next page. If a worksheet is copied or moved in this way, any formulas will stay exactly as they were in the original sheet.

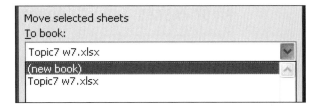

using Copy and Paste to move data

Moving or copying a worksheet as described above is an easy way of moving data from one worksheet to another, whether in the same or in different workbooks.

It is also possible to use the normal Copy and Paste to copy all or part of the data from a worksheet in one open workbook to a worksheet in another open workbook. In the image below, you can see the bank transaction data with the workbook filename **Topic7 w7** at the top of the image.

	A	B	C	D	E	F
1	Bank transactions					
2						
3	Opening balance	1,500.00				
4	Closing balance	1,289.05				
5	Adjustment	17.00				
6	New balance					
7						
8	**Date**	**Debit**	**Credit**	**Balance**		
9	02/07/2010	95.34	0.00	1,404.66		
10	11/07/2010	0.00	25.50	1,430.16		
11	15/07/2010	0.00	34.78	1,464.94		
12	22/07/2010	67.90	0.00	1,397.04		
13	28/07/2010	107.99	0.00	1,289.05		
14	**Totals**	271.23	60.28		1,289.05	

Sheets: **July** / Adjust

Suppose we want to copy some of the transaction data to a worksheet in another workbook (filename Book5). To do this we select cells A8:C13, and **Copy and Paste** onto **sheet1** in the other workbook, as shown below.

Book5

	A	B	C
1	**Date**	**Debit**	**Credit**
2	02/07/2010	95.34	0.00
3	11/07/2010	0.00	25.50
4	15/07/2010	0.00	34.78
5	22/07/2010	67.90	0.00
6	28/07/2010	107.99	0.00
7	**Totals**	271.23	60.28

Sheets: **Sheet1** / Sheet

PIVOT TABLES – AN INTRODUCTION

what is a pivot table?

A **Pivot table** is a very powerful reporting feature found in spreadsheet packages. Pivot tables allow us to generate and extract meaningful information from a large table of information within a matter of minutes, by creating an interactive summary from a worksheet containing numerous rows. This summary is known as a **pivot table**.

advantages of a pivot table

Instead of having to analyse vast amounts of data, a pivot table can sort, count, subtotal and total your numeric information. It can allow you to look at the data in different ways very quickly and easily.

It is possible to expand and collapse levels of data and drill down to details from the summary data to look at areas in more detail.

Changing the format in which the data is summarised, by moving rows to columns or columns to rows (pivoting) allows you to see different summaries of the same source data.

examples of pivot tables

If we look at the image below, we can see a small part of some extended sales data relating to the sales generated by individual sales reps:

	A	B	C	D	E	F
1	Sales					
2						
3	Month	Product	Value	Sales Rep	Country	
4	Jan	Accessories	£125.75	TP	IND	
5	Jan	Footwear	£99.95	SM	PKN	
6	Jan	Luggage	£220.00	IY	GER	
7	Jan	Luggage	£1,400.00	MP	UK	
8	Jan	Luggage	£1,400.00	MP	UK	
9	Feb	Jewellery	£1,500.00	TP	UK	
10	Feb	Footwear	£220.00	IY	FR	
11	Feb	Jewellery	£67.75	IO	GER	
12	Feb	Clothing	£34.90	SM	SP	
13	Mar	Footwear	£154.50	IY	GER	
14	Mar	Luggage	£124.60	SM	SP	

In the example pivot table on the next page we are showing for each sales rep, the value of each product type sold (eg Accessories, Clothing etc) created from the sales data, and summarised in a simple table.

	A	B	C	D	E	F	G	H
1								
2								
3	Sum of Value	Product ▾						
4	Sales Rep ▾	Accessories	Clothing	Footwear	Jewellery	Luggage	Other	Grand Total
5	IY	£1,585	£45	£375	£126	£220	£4,706	£7,056
6	IO	£335	£1,180		£183	£553	£1,647	£3,897
7	MP	£125		£253	£34	£2,800		£3,212
8	SM		£444	£225	£240	£192		£1,101
9	TP	£214	£100	£1,586	£1,500		£125	£3,524
10	Grand Total	£2,258	£1,769	£2,438	£2,083	£3,765	£6,478	£18,790

If we then wanted to see the detail of the Accessories sales made by sales rep IY, we could select cell B5, and 'drill down' and extract this detail, as can be seen in the image below.

	A	B	C	D	E	F
1	Month ▾	Product ▾	Value ▾	Sales Rep ▾	Country ▾	
2	Nov	Accessories	56	IY	FR	
3	Oct	Accessories	34.9	IY	PKN	
4	Sep	Accessories	34	IY	GER	
5	Sep	Accessories	1460.4	IY	FR	
6						
7						
8						
9						
10						
11						

Drill down / Sheet4 / Sheet1 / Sheet2 / Sheet3

You can see that the table provides a very powerful analysis and reporting tool.

We will now explain how to set up pivot tables in a worksheet.

CREATING A PIVOT TABLE

The techniques for creating a pivot table will vary greatly between spreadsheet packages, and even between versions of the same package, but the principles remain the same. In the steps that follow we will be creating a table in Microsoft® Excel version 2010.

We will work with the sales data used in the examples above.

Step 1 - Setting up the data

The data should be set out in columns going down the worksheet.

The columns of data should be adjacent, and start in the same row.

Each column of data should have a title (name) which relates to the data it contains. In our example we have the following titles:

- Month
- Product
- Value
- Sales Rep
- Country

These titles are normal pieces of text and should be placed in the cell directly above the first data cell, for each column.

The titles are also known as **fields** (of data) within the pivot table environment and are used extensively in the creation of a pivot table.

Step 2 – Selecting the data

Select all your data, including the column titles.

Step 3 – Creating the pivot table

Select the **PivotTable** tool from the appropriate menu.

The following message box should appear:

Check that the range entered in the **Table/Range** box is correct and includes all your data cells.

Leave the **New Worksheet** button selected – this will automatically create the pivot table on a new worksheet within your current workbook.

Select OK to continue.

Step 4 – Laying out your table

Once we have selected OK, a screen similar to the one below is displayed. (This may vary, depending on the way your package is set up. This classic **PivotTable** layout can be obtained by selecting **Options** within the **PivotTable** menu, select **Display** and select **Classic PivotTable** layout.) It shows the default options when we start to create the table.

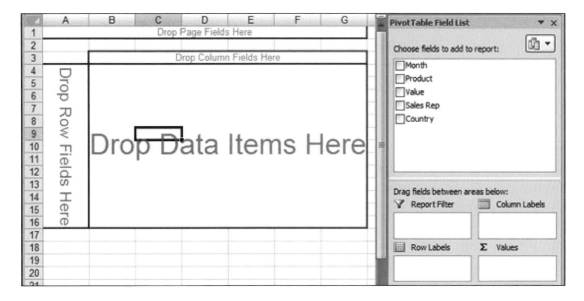

You can see our list of column titles (fields) in the small box (**Fields List**) top right, and a layout template across the cells of the worksheet.

In our example we are going to calculate the value of sales for each **country** by **product**. These are the two fields of data which we want to display.

We want to have:

■ products in columns

■ countries in rows

All we have to do is select the appropriate fields, one at a time from the fields list (top right), and drag them across to the layout template, or to the **Column Labels** or **Row Labels** boxes below the field list.

We will first select the country field from the **Field List**, and drag to the **Row Fields** section (shown in column A in the image above) and release.

The layout immediately changes to reflect this, as shown on the next page.

You can see that the different **countries** from our sales data are displayed in column A, one row for each country, sorted alphabetically, and with a Grand Total at the bottom.

In the **Field List** box, the **Country** field is now ticked to indicate that we have selected it.

Now we select the **Product** field from the **Field List**, and drag it to the Column Fields section (shown in rows 3 and 4 in the image above) and release. The screen then appears as shown below.

You can see that the titles for the different products from within our data are displayed in Row 4, starting from Column B. There is one column for each product, sorted alphabetically, and with a Grand Total at the end. In the Field List box, the product field is now ticked to indicate that we have selected it.

As you can see, the layout structure is becoming clearer. One further step is now required to include the sales value data so that we can analyse the sales.

To include this field, we select the **Value** field from the **Field List**, and drag it to the **Drop Data Items Here** area in the layout template and then release.

As our pivot table has now taken shape, we can close the Field List box on the right hand side of the screen. If you want the box visible again, just select it from the pivot table menu.

We have our first simple pivot table – the **value** of sales for each **country** by **product** as can be seen in the image below.

Sum of Value	Product						
Country	Accessories	Clothing	Footwear	Jewellery	Luggage	Other	Grand Total
CHN		44.75		120		191.15	355.9
FR	1516.4	1180	220	125.75		2960.4	6002.55
GER	271.1		407.5	187.75	332.5	56.25	1255.1
IND	125.75	99.95					281.95
JPN	67.75				220		287.75
PKN	34.9		99.95		67.75	1554	1756.6
SP	154.5	34.9	124.6	149	344.6	1534.9	2342.5
UK	88	408.95	1586.15	1500	2800	124.6	6507.7
Grand Total	2258.4	1768.55	2438.2	2082.5	3764.85	6477.55	18790.05

REMOVING OR CHANGING A PIVOT TABLE

changing fields

If you want to **change** which fields you are including in the pivot table, you can select it from the pivot table and drag it back to the field list box.

For example, to take the country field out of the table on the next page:

■ select cell A4, which holds the field name **Country**

■ drag field name **Country** back to the field list box.

	A	B	C	D	E	F	G	H
1								
2								
3	Sum of Value	Product ▾						
4	Country ▾	Accessories	Clothing	Footwear	Jewellery	Luggage	Other	Grand Total
5	CHN		44.75		120		191.15	355.9
6	FR	1516.4	1180	220	125.75		2960.4	6002.55
7	GER	271.1		407.5	187.75	332.5	56.25	1255.1
8	IND	125.75	99.95				56.25	281.95
9	JPN	67.75				220		287.75
10	PKN	34.9		99.95		67.75	1554	1756.6
11	SP	154.5	34.9	124.6	149	344.6	1534.9	2342.5
12	UK	88	408.95	1586.15	1500	2800	124.6	6507.7
13	Grand Total	2258.4	1768.55	2438.2	2082.5	3764.85	6477.55	18790.05
14								

clearing a pivot table

If you have started or created a pivot table, and you want to clear what you have done and start again:

■ select **Clear** from the pivot table menu

■ select **Clear All** from the drop down

FORMATTING PIVOT TABLES

There are a variety of ways in which you can change the format or appearance of your table.

cell display

To change the way individual data values are displayed within the table, you can use the standard cell formatting options described in Chapters 2 and 3.

In the pivot table created in this chapter, our sales values are displayed as decimal numbers, rather than the £ (UK pound) currency. To change this:

■ select all the numeric data cells, including the Grand Total row and column

■ select **Format Cells**,

■ select **Currency**, with the pound (£) symbol, and 2 decimal places

table style

Within the pivot table Design Menu there are a variety of styles which can be used for the table layout, colouring, and shading, all of which change the appearance of the table.

It is also possible to change other factors affecting the layout, for example row headers, column headers, subtotals and grand totals. This is an area where it is recommended that you experiment within your spreadsheet package to find your preferred style.

subsets of data

The pivot table we have created includes all the countries and products found within our data set.

It is possible that we may not want to include all values of one or other field. Suppose we only wanted to include countries FR, GER, SP and UK in our pivot table to show European sales values. This is easily achieved as follows:

- select the drop down symbol to the right of the Country field (cell A4)

- deselect CHN, IND, JPN, PKN from the list (as shown below)

- select OK

The pivot table adjusts to reflect these choices, as shown in the image below. This technique is a quick and easy way of displaying a **subset** of the data.

	A	B	C	D	E	F	G	H
1								
2								
3	Sum of Value	Product ⏷						
4	Country ⏷	Accessories	Clothing	Footwear	Jewellery	Luggage	Other	Grand Total
5	FR	£1,516.40	£1,180.00	£220.00	£125.75		£2,960.40	£6,002.55
6	GER	£271.10		£407.50	£187.75	£332.50	£56.25	£1,255.10
7	SP	£154.50	£34.90	£124.60	£149.00	£344.60	£1,534.90	£2,342.50
8	UK	£88.00	£408.95	£1,586.15	£1,500.00	£2,800.00	£124.60	£6,507.70
9	Grand Total	£2,030.00	£1,623.85	£2,338.25	£1,962.50	£3,477.10	£4,676.15	£16,107.85
10								

DRILL DOWN

The term '**drill down**' is frequently used when analysing data and is used to describe the ability to display the underlying data values which make up a total or subtotal.

In the sales pivot table created in this chapter, if we wanted to see which individual sales made up £1516.40 value of **Accessories** sales in **FR**, we would move to cell B5 which shows the total value for Accessories sales in FR. We then double click with the mouse on this cell. The detail making up this total is displayed on a fresh worksheet, as can be seen in the image below. This shows that when we **drill down** into the data, we can see that there were two sales of £1,460.40 and £56.00 making up this value of £1,516.40.

Note when you do a **drill down** there is, by default, no automatic formatting of data. As you can see in the Value column below, for example, the money amounts do not have '£' signs or a fixed number of decimal places. These can be formatted subsequently as required (see the screen image on the next page).

column C before formatting

	A	B	C	D	E	F
1	Month ⏷	Product ⏷	Value ⏷	Who ⏷	Country ⏷	
2	Sep	Accessories	1460.4	IY	FR	
3	Nov	Accessories	56	IY	FR	
4						
5						
6						

column C after formatting

	A	B	C	D	E	F
1	Month ▾	Product ▾	Value ▾	Who ▾	Country ▾	
2	Sep	Accessories	£1,460.40	IY	FR	
3	Nov	Accessories	£56.00	IY	FR	
4						
5						
6						

WHAT-IF SCENARIOS

Spreadsheets are created to serve many purposes. One use is to have Excel analyse what the result would be if we applied different sets of values to one or more formulas. A simple example might be to see how different interest rates might change the loan repayments, and subsequently the profit, of a business. This could be achieved by having the interest rate built into a formula and manually changing it one value at a time, as required. However Excel provides a powerful tool which allows us to offer up multiple scenarios and then automatically produce a report showing the various outcomes – these are known as **What-If scenarios**.

In the example below, we have a simple summary showing the calculated profit, based on a loan interest repayment rate of 15% and expected sales of €200,000. Cell B15 contains the formula necessary to calculate the profit.

We want to see the effect on profit if we have higher or lower interest rates, or if sales don't meet our expectations.

	A	B	C
1	Example What If Scenarios		
2			
3	Interest Rate (%)	15	
4	Loan	€ 100,000	
5			
6	Sales	€ 200,000	
7			
8	Loan Repayments	€ 15,000	
9	Salaries	€ 90,000	
10	Insurance	€ 2,500	
11	Rent	€ 19,080	
12	Advertising	€ 20,000	
13	Other	€ 19,950	
14			
15	Profit	€33,470	
16			

To achieve this we will create our first scenario as follows:

- select **What-If analysis** from the Data menu

- select **Scenario Manager**

- select **Add**

- **scenario name** enter High Interest

- **changing cells** enter or select B3 and B6 separated by commas (the cells containing the values for the interest rate and sales)

Now we enter the **values** for these cells for this scenario

- enter 20 for B3 leave B6 unchanged and click OK

We now select **Add** (another scenario)

- **scenario name** enter Low Interest

- continue as before and enter 10 as the value for B3

Create two more scenarios; Poor Sales using cell B6 and a value of €150,000, and High Interest Poor Sales using cells B3 and B6 with values of 20 and €150,000 respectively.

The list of scenarios should appear as shown below:

Now that we have defined the scenarios we wish to consider, we select **summary** to produce a report. This can take the form of a scenario summary or a PivotTable report. We also define the **Result** cell, which in this case will be B15 (the profit cell). We select **Scenario summary** and get the table shown below.

Scenario Summary	Current Values:	High Interest	Low Interest	Poor Sales	High Interest Poor Sales
Changing Cells:					
$B$3	15	20	10	15	20
$B$6	€ 200,000	€ 200,000	€ 200,000	€ 150,000	€ 150,000
Result Cells:					
$B$15	€ 33,470	€ 28,470	€ 38,470	-€ 16,530	-€ 21,530

This summary is showing us the values we can expect for profit for the different interest rates and forecast sales.

goal seek

Another tool within the **What-If analysis toolpak** is **Goal Seek**. This tool allows us to specify an outcome which we require, for example a profit of €40,000, and then a value (cell) which can be changed by the tool to achieve this outcome. So using our profit example above we want to know how big a loan we could take out, assuming an interest rate of 15% and sales of €200,000 to achieve a profit of €40,000.

To do this:

■ select **What-If Analysis**

■ select **Goal Seek**

And the Goal Seek option box is displayed as shown below:

	A	B	C	D	E	F
1	Example What If Scenarios					
2						
3	Interest Rate (%)	15				
4	Loan	€ 100,000				
5						
6	Sales	€ 200,000				
7						
8	Loan Repayments	€ 15,000				
9	Salaries	€ 90,000				
10	Insurance	€ 2,500				
11	Rent	€ 19,080				
12	Advertising	€ 20,000				
13	Other	€ 19,950				
14						
15	Profit	€ 33,470				

Goal Seek

Set cell: $B$15

To value: 40000

By changing cell: $B$4

OK   Cancel

The **Set cell** is B15, the cell containing the profit value, and the **To value** is €40,000 the profit we want to achieve. We allow the loan value cell B4 to change, in order to achieve this profit.

	A	B	C	D	E	F
1	Example What If Scenarios					
2						
3	Interest Rate (%)	15				
4	Loan	€ 56,467				
5						
6	Sales	€ 200,000				
7						
8	Loan Repayments	€ 8,470				
9	Salaries	€ 90,000				
10	Insurance	€ 2,500				
11	Rent	€ 19,080				
12	Advertising	€ 20,000				
13	Other	€ 19,950				
14						
15	Profit	€ 40,000				

Goal Seek Status

Goal Seeking with Cell B15 found a solution.

Target value: 40000
Current value: € 40,000

Step | Pause | OK | Cancel

This shows that a solution has been found, a loan value of €56,467 would achieve a profit of €40,000.

data tables

The final tool in the **What-If Analysis toolpak** is **Data Tables**, which provide us with the ability to change one or two variables in one or more of our formulas to a series of different (test) values. These test values are supplied as a series, in a row or column. Data tables provide an easy way of calculating multiple results in one operation and to then view and compare the results of all the different variations together in one place.

To illustrate the use of **Data Tables** we are going to look at a simple example shown in the image below.

	A	B
1	Example Data Tables	
2		
3	Sales	€ 200,000
4	Annual growth in Sales	2.00%
5	Predicted Sales	€ 204,000

We have our current Sales figures for the year of €200,000. We are predicting growth in sales of 2%. From this we insert a formula in cell B5 to calculate our Predicted Sales. Now we will insert our series of growth values to be evaluated.

◢	A	B	C	D	E	F	G	H	I	J
1	Example Data Tables									
2										
3	Sales	€ 200,000								
4	Annual growth in Sales	2.00%	1.0%	1.2%	1.4%	1.6%	1.8%	2.2%	2.4%	2.6%
5	Predicted Sales	€ 204,000								

To use **Data Tables**:

■ select cells B4 through to J5 (this is to include our formula in cell B5 and our series of values)

■ select **What-If Analysis**

■ select **Data Tables**

◢	A	B	C	D	E	F	G	H	I	J
1	Example Data Tables									
2										
3	Sales	€ 200,000								
4	Annual growth in Sales	2.00%	1.0%	1.2%	1.4%	1.6%	1.8%	2.2%	2.4%	2.6%
5	Predicted Sales	€ 204,000								
6										
7										
8										
9										
10										
11										

Data Table

Row input cell: $B$4

Column input cell:

OK   Cancel

The **Data Table** options are then displayed. We have put our series of values along a row, so we specify a **Row input cell** (and not a **Column Input** cell). The cell we specify is B4, the cell containing out current sales growth %. When we click OK, the table is completed and Predicted Sales figures are generated for each of the growth values, as can be seen in the image below.

◢	A	B	C	D	E	F	G	H	I	J
1	Example Data Tables									
2										
3	Sales	€ 200,000								
4	Annual growth in Sales	2.00%	1.0%	1.2%	1.4%	1.6%	1.8%	2.2%	2.4%	2.6%
5	Predicted Sales	€ 204,000	€ 202,000	€ 202,400	€ 202,800	€ 203,200	€ 203,600	€ 204,400	€ 204,800	€ 205,200

If you select one of the Predicted Sales cells, you see that the formula for the cell shows that it is part of a table based on cell B4, as shown below.

E5 f_x {=TABLE(B4,)}

◢	A	B	C	D	E	F	G	H	I	J
1	Example Data Tables									
2										
3	Sales	€ 200,000								
4	Annual growth in Sales	2.00%	1.0%	1.2%	1.4%	1.6%	1.8%	2.2%	2.4%	2.6%
5	Predicted Sales	€ 204,000	€ 202,000	€ 202,400	€ 202,800	€ 203,200	€ 203,600	€ 204,400	€ 204,800	€ 205,200

As can be seen in the **Data Table** options, the series of values can be in a column instead of a row. It is also possible to have 2 items that change, a series in a row and a series in a column. We will not be covering 2 dimensional Data Tables, and recommend that you experiment further.

Note: If the series is in a row, the formula to be calculated should be in the row below the series, and for columns, the formula should be in the column to the right of the series.

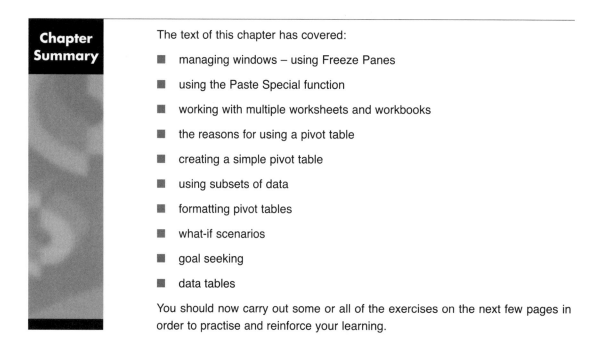

Chapter Summary

The text of this chapter has covered:

- managing windows – using Freeze Panes

- using the Paste Special function

- working with multiple worksheets and workbooks

- the reasons for using a pivot table

- creating a simple pivot table

- using subsets of data

- formatting pivot tables

- what-if scenarios

- goal seeking

- data tables

You should now carry out some or all of the exercises on the next few pages in order to practise and reinforce your learning.

Activities

Exercise 1 – using Freeze Panes

In this first exercise we will use the **window – Freeze Panes** facility.

To obtain this spreadsheet visit www.osbornebooks.co.uk ('Resources') and download filename **T7freeze**.

Stage 1

This stage uses the **Freeze Panes** and **Unfreeze** facilities to enable us to scroll around a sales spreadsheet with a large amount of data, and still be able to interpret the data.

1.   Download the workbook **T7freeze**

2.   Open the downloaded file, save the workbook with new name **T7Exercise1**

The top section of the workbook should look as shown below.

	A	B	C	D	E	F	G	H	I	J	K
1	Name	Total	Month1	Month2	Month3	Month4	Month5	Month6	Month7	Month8	Month9
2	Farmhouse Foods	£154	£0	£112	£0	£0	£0	£26	£0	£0	£16
3	Engineering Services	£554	£0	£0	£0	£0	£67	£0	£0	£0	£0
4	Another Food Service	£790	£0	£0	£0	£58	£116	£0	£0	£174	£0
5	Top Quality Supplies	£56	£0	£56	£0	£0	£0	£0	£0	£0	£0
6	Halal Foods	£36	£0	£0	£0	£0	£0	£0	£0	£0	£0
7	Edwards Farm	£195	£0	£0	£0	£0	£40	£0	£65	£0	£0
8	Allen and co	£1,412	£45	£68	£231	£0	£331	£37	£49	£0	£0
9	Ahmed and son	£340	£0	£0	£0	£0	£0	£0	£0	£0	£0
10	Green & Sons Wholesalers	£1,827	£700	£0	£104	£0	£0	£0	£0	£0	£363
11	Higginbottom and son	£389	£0	£0	£0	£0	£0	£0	£300	£0	£0
12	W B Meats	£135	£0	£45	£0	£0	£0	£0	£0	£0	£0
13	The Halal Centre	£205	£0	£0	£50	£0	£0	£0	£0	£25	£0
14	T F Curries	£7,245	£458	£166	£583	£225	£414	£365	£470	£490	£244
15	Fiber Optical Services	£90	£0	£40	£0	£0	£0	£0	£0	£0	£0

Customer Sales / Sheet2 / Sheet3 / 💲

3.   Select the appropriate cell, and then **Freeze Panes**, so that the column headings in Row 1 stay in view when you scroll down the worksheet, and the row headings in Column A stay in view when you scroll across.

4.   Using the normal scrolling facilities scroll the view, so that cell I14 (T F Curries, Month7 value) becomes the top left-hand cell in the viewing area.

Your worksheet should look as shown at the top of the next page.

A	I	J	K	L	M	N	O
1 Name	Month7	Month8	Month9	Month10	Month11	Month12	Month13
14 T F Curries	£470	£490	£244	£423	£354	£560	£309
15 Fiber Optical Services	£0	£0	£0	£0	£0	£0	£0
16 My Provisions	£0	£25	£0	£0	£0	£0	£0
17 Alliance services	£0	£0	£0	£0	£0	£0	£0
18 Aluminium casts	£72	£286	£0	£2,093	£0	£364	£1,750
19 Impala	£0	£0	£0	£0	£0	£0	£0
20 Tool Hire	£0	£0	£0	£0	£0	£0	£0
21 Handyfreight	£0	£0	£0	£0	£0	£0	£327
22 Steel Traders	£0	£0	£0	£0	£0	£0	£0
23 Fruit Supplies	£0	£0	£65	£0	£279	£0	£0
24 Food Safe	£0	£55	£0	£0	£0	£0	£0
25 Environmental Services	£112	£0	£112	£0	£140	£0	£0

H ◀ ▶ H **Customer Sales** Sheet2 Sheet3

5. We now want to freeze panes so that we can visually compare the figures in Month1, and the figures in Month7.

Unfreeze Panes, then select the appropriate cell, then **Freeze Panes**.

Then scroll to the top of your spreadsheet and scroll the view until Month7 (column I) is next to Month1 (column C).

Your worksheet should look as shown below.

A	B	C	I	J	K	L	M	N
1 Name	Total	Month1	Month7	Month8	Month9	Month10	Month11	Month12
2 Farmhouse Foods	£154	£0	£0	£0	£16	£0	£0	£0
3 Engineering Services	£554	£0	£0	£0	£0	£0	£0	£0
4 Another Food Service	£790	£0	£0	£174	£0	£0	£0	£0
5 Top Quality Supplies	£56	£0	£0	£0	£0	£0	£0	£0
6 Halal Foods	£36	£0	£0	£0	£0	£0	£36	£0
7 Edwards Farm	£195	£0	£65	£0	£0	£0	£0	£90
8 Allen and co	£1,412	£45	£49	£0	£0	£100	£115	£77
9 Ahmed and son	£340	£0	£0	£0	£0	£0	£0	£0
10 Green & Sons Wholesalers	£1,827	£700	£0	£0	£363	£0	£0	£0
11 Higginbottom and son	£389	£0	£300	£0	£0	£0	£89	£0
12 W B Meats	£135	£0	£0	£0	£0	£0	£0	£0
13 The Halal Centre	£205	£0	£0	£25	£0	£0	£0	£0
14 T F Curries	£7,245	£458	£470	£490	£244	£423	£354	£560
15 Fiber Optical Services	£90	£0	£0	£0	£0	£0	£0	£0

H ◀ ▶ H **Customer Sales** Sheet2 Sheet3

6. We now want to freeze panes so that we can visually compare the figures for Allen and co (row 8), and the figures for T F Curries (row 14). **Unfreeze Panes**, then select the appropriate cell, then **Freeze Panes**, then using the normal scrolling facilities, scroll the view until T F Curries is next to Allen and co.

Your worksheet should look as shown at the top of the next page.

	A	B	C	D	E	F	G	H	I	
1	Name	Total	Month1	Month2	Month3	Month4	Month5	Month6	Month7	Mo
2	Farmhouse Foods	£154	£0	£112	£0	£0	£0	£26	£0	
3	Engineering Services	£554	£0	£0	£0	£0	£67	£0	£0	
4	Another Food Service	£790	£0	£0	£0	£58	£116	£0	£0	
5	Top Quality Supplies	£56	£0	£56	£0	£0	£0	£0	£0	
6	Halal Foods	£36	£0	£0	£0	£0	£0	£0	£0	
7	Edwards Farm	£195	£0	£0	£0	£0	£40	£0	£65	
8	Allen and co	£1,412	£45	£68	£231	£0	£331	£37	£49	
14	T F Curries	£7,245	£458	£166	£583	£225	£414	£365	£470	
15	Fiber Optical Services	£90	£0	£40	£0	£0	£0	£0	£0	
16	My Provisions	£75	£0	£0	£0	£0	£0	£0	£0	
17	Alliance services	£327	£0	£0	£0	£0	£0	£0	£0	
18	Aluminium casts	£7,625	£72	£54	£1,856	£0	£360	£119	£72	
19	Impala	£143	£0	£0	£0	£0	£0	£98	£0	
20	Tool Hire	£35	£0	£0	£15	£0	£0	£0	£0	

Customer Sales / Sheet2 / Sheet3

7. Save the workbook with the same name **T7Exercise1**

You have now completed the first exercise.

Exercise 2 – Paste Special, multiple worksheets and workbooks

In this exercise we will work with **Paste Special**, move data and formulas from **one worksheet to another** and across **multiple workbooks**, and also use the **Move or Copy Sheet** facility. We are again going to make use of an existing spreadsheet, containing data relating to monthly car sales.

To obtain this spreadsheet visit www.osbornebooks.co.uk ('Resources') and download filename **T7paste**

Stage 1

This stage uses **Paste Special** and requires you to move data and formulas from one worksheet to another.

1. Download the workbook **T7paste**

2. Open the downloaded file, save the workbook with new name **T7Exercise2**

3. The workbook should look as shown below. You can see that the formula for the Total for the Ford row (row 6), in cell B6 is, as we would expect:

   =SUM(C6:H6)

	A	B	C	D	E	F	G	H	I	J
1	Car Sales									
2										
3			Max	60,000	Min	930	Count	42		
4									Average	
5		Totals	Jan	Feb	Mar	Apr	May	Jun	3 month	6 month
6	Ford	190,000	25,090	25,000	60,000	25,010	30,900	24,000	24,670	31,667
7	Volkswagen	98,510	13,200	6,150	32,900	15,130	15,040	16,090	12,457	16,418
8	Hyundai	9,000	1,000	1,500	2,500	1,000	1,000	2,000	1,500	1,500
9	Skoda	15,400	1,200	2,800	4,000	3,500	2,130	1,770	2,690	2,567
10	Kia	13,360	930	1,050	5,430	1,500	2,110	2,340	1,630	2,227
11	Renault	94,820	7,000	32,090	25,600	9,230	9,100	11,800	17,707	15,803
12	Vauxhall	166,750	22,000	10,500	55,000	25,050	24,100	30,100	21,883	27,792

4. Change the name of worksheet Sheet1 to **Car Sales**.

5. Check that you have a second worksheet in the workbook you have open; if not add a worksheet (as described in Chapter 1) and name it **Copy1**.

6. Select all the data on the Car Sales worksheet, select **Copy** (using the menu, or **CTRL** and **C**)

7. Select worksheet **Copy1**, move to cell B2, select **Paste Special** (from the menu), select **All**, the data from **Car Sales** will be pasted onto the worksheet **Copy1**.

8. On worksheet **Copy1**, make Column A four units wide.

9. On worksheet **Copy1**, move to cell C7. You should see the formula for the Total for the Ford row (now Row 7 on this sheet):

=SUM(D7:I7)

This will have been modified to reflect the new row and column position, as shown in the image below.

10. Save your spreadsheet (keeping the same name – **T7Exercise2**).

	A	B	C	D	E	F	G	H	I	J	K
1											
2		Car Sales									
3											
4				Max	60,000	Min	930	Count	42		
5										Average	
6			Totals	Jan	Feb	Mar	Apr	May	Jun	3 month	6 month
7		Ford	190,000	25,090	25,000	60,000	25,010	30,900	24,000	24,670	31,667
8		Volkswagen	98,510	13,200	6,150	32,900	15,130	15,040	16,090	12,457	16,418
9		Hyundai	9,000	1,000	1,500	2,500	1,000	1,000	2,000	1,500	1,500
10		Skoda	15,400	1,200	2,800	4,000	3,500	2,130	1,770	2,690	2,567
11		Kia	13,360	930	1,050	5,430	1,500	2,110	2,340	1,630	2,227
12		Renault	94,820	7,000	32,090	25,600	9,230	9,100	11,800	17,707	15,803
13		Vauxhall	166,750	22,000	10,500	55,000	25,050	24,100	30,100	21,883	27,792

Stage 2

In this stage we are going to use **Paste Special, Values**. You should use the same workbook **T7Exercise2**.

1. Check that you have a third worksheet in the workbook, if not add a worksheet (as described in Chapter 1) and name it **Copy2**.

2. Select worksheet **Copy2**, format Column B to be **Bold** and **Italics**, format Column C to be **Currency pounds (£)** and with **2 decimal places**.

3. Select the data in Columns A and B on the Car Sales worksheet, select **Copy** (using either the menu, or **CTRL** and **C**)

4. Select worksheet **Copy2**, move to cell B2, select **Paste Special**, select **Values**.

5. On worksheet **Copy2**, make Column A 2 units wide, widen Column C so that all the data is displayed, Delete rows 3 and 4.

6. On worksheet **Copy2**, move to cell C5. There is no longer a formula for the **Total** for the Ford row (now row 5 on this sheet), only the value that was produced by the original calculation. You can also see that the cell formatting has been changed to the format we put in place on worksheet **Copy2**, as shown in the image on the next page.

	C5		f_x	190000	

	A	B	C	D	E	F
1						
2		Car Sales				
3						
4			Totals			
5		Ford	£190,000.00			
6		Volkswagen	£98,510.00			
7		Hyundai	£9,000.00			
8		Skoda	£15,400.00			
9		Kia	£13,360.00			
10		Renault	£94,820.00			
11		Vauxhall	£166,750.00			
12						

Car sales / Copy1 / Copy2

7.   Save your spreadsheet (keeping the same name – **T7Exercise2**.

Stage 3

In this stage we are going to use **Paste Special**, **Formats** within the same workbook, **T7Exercise2**.

We will change the format of the data on **Copy2** by copying the format from the original Car Sales worksheet

1.   Select worksheet **Car Sales**, select cells **B6:B12** select **Copy**.

2.   Select worksheet **Copy2**, move to cell C5, select **Paste Special**, select **Formats**.

3.   On worksheet **Copy2**, you can also see that the cell formatting of the totals cells (C5:C11) has been changed back to the format from worksheet **Car Sales**: there are no pound symbols or decimal places showing pence. The screen will appear as shown below.

4.   Save your spreadsheet (keeping the same name – **T7Exercise2**).

	C5		f_x	190000	

	A	B	C	D	E	F
1						
2		Car Sales				
3						
4			Totals			
5		Ford	190,000			
6		Volkswagen	98,510			
7		Hyundai	9,000			
8		Skoda	15,400			
9		Kia	13,360			
10		Renault	94,820			
11		Vauxhall	166,750			
12						

Car sales / Copy1 / Copy2

Stage 4

In this stage, we are going to create some formulas which reference a specific worksheet.

We will then copy the formulas from one workbook to another, using **Copy and Paste** and **Paste Special**.

We will make use of the same workbook **T7Exercise2**, and also create a new workbook to which we will copy data.

1. Check that you have a fourth worksheet in the workbook, if not, add a worksheet (as described in Chapter 1) and name it **Copy3**.

2. Select the data in Rows 1, 2 and 3 on the **Car Sales** worksheet, select **Copy** (using either the menu, or **CTRL** and **C**)

3. Select worksheet **Copy3**, move to cell A1, select **Paste Special**, select **All**.

You will see that the values for **Max**, **Min** and **Count** are now zero, since we did not copy all the values which they reference. Rather than copy these values, we are going to link directly to the cells which held the results on worksheet **Car Sales**.

4. On worksheet **Copy3**, move to cell D3, enter the = (to indicate a formula), move to worksheet **Car Sales**, select cell D3, press **ENTER**.

    You should now see the value for **Max** from Car Sales displayed, and the formula includes a direct reference to the Car Sales worksheet.

5. Repeat for **Min** and **Count**.

6. Save your workbook as **T7Exercise2**.

The Copy3 worksheet should now look as shown in the image below.

7. Open a new workbook, save it with name **T7Excopy**, name the first worksheet **Sheet1** (if it is not already called that).

8. Select workbook **T7Exercise2**, worksheet **Copy3**, select all the data on the worksheet, select **Copy**.

9. Select workbook **T7Excopy**, worksheet **Sheet1**, select cell A1, select **Paste**. The data from **Copy3** will be pasted onto the worksheet **Sheet1**.

10. On worksheet **Sheet1**, select **Show Formulas**.

11. By adjusting the column widths, you can see the formulas as shown in the image below.

	D3				f_x	='[T7Exercise2.xlsx]Car sales'!D3			
	A	B	C	D	E	F	G	H
1	Car Sales							
2								
3			Max	='[T7Exercise2.xlsx]Car sales'!D3	Min	='[T7Exercise2.xlsx]Car sales'!F3	Count	='[T7Exercise2.xlsx]Car
4								
5								
6								
7								

You can see that the formulas in the new workbook contain direct references to the workbook containing the original data. If we did not want to retain the link to the original worksheet, we would use **Paste Special** and **Values**.

You have now completed Exercise 2.

Exercise 3 – using pivot tables

In this exercise we are going to create a pivot table, from some data in a prepared file, which can be downloaded from the Osborne books website, filename **T7pivot**. We are also going to practise using **Move or Copy Sheet**.

To obtain this spreadsheet visit www.osbornebooks.co.uk ('Resources') and download filename **T7pivot**

Stage 1

1.   Download the workbook **T7pivot**

2.   Open the downloaded file, save the workbook with new name **T7Exercise3**

3.   The top few rows of the workbook should look as shown below.

	A	B	C	D	E	F	G
1							
2		*Products*	*Quantity*	*Month*	*Value*		
3		Product1	3,063	Jan	£3,115.90		
4		Product2	406	Jan	£614.50		
5		Product3	192	Jan	£1,646.50		
6		Product4	97	Jan	£600.00		
7		Product6	47	Jan	£106.90		
8		Product6	13	Jan	£160.00		
9		Product1	4,661	Jan	£8,801.70		
10		Product2	975	Feb	£416.10		
11		Product3	407	Feb	£260.80		
12		Product4	163	Feb	£1,147.50		
13		Product5	128	Feb	£1,100.00		

Sheet1 / Sheet2 / Sheet3

We are now going to create a pivot table to allow us to look at product sales quantities by month.

4.   Select all the data in the worksheet, including the column titles (Row 2).

5.   Select the **PivotTable** tool from the menu.

6.   In the **Create PivotTable** options choose **Select a table or range**. This should display the full range of the data on the worksheet ie **Sheet1!$B$2:$E$86**. (Edit if necessary so that this is the range selected).

7.   In the **Create PivotTable** options, select **New Worksheet**, and then **OK**

8.   Select the **Products Field** as the row field/labels.

9.   Select the **Month Field** as the column field/labels.

10.   Select the **Quantity Field** as the values field.

11.   Save your workbook as **T7Exercise3**.

The pivot table showing product sales quantities by month should then appear on a new worksheet, as shown in the image below (possibly with different shading or colours).

	A	B	C	D	E	F	G	H	I	J	K	L	M	N
1														
2														
3	Sum of Quantity	Column Labels ▾												
4	Row Labels ▾	Jan	Feb	Mar	Apr	May	Jun	Jul	Aug	Sep	Oct	Nov	Dec	Grand Total
5	Product1	7724	15		125	856	3703	1383	13		257	429	2993	17498
6	Product2	406	10558	41		1281	1584	1763	5014	71		333	186	21237
7	Product3	192	407	33539	1972		17	2202	3055	27197	54		350	68985
8	Product4	97	163	279	7076	9		746	1243	2472	13251	15		25351
9	Product5		145	237	200	3026	38		212	273	356	355	2	4844
10	Product6	60		584	784	341	478	-40		127	288	2757	2360	7739
11	Grand Total		8479	11288	34680	10157	5513	5820	6054	9537	30140	14206	3889	5891	145654

12. Using the pivot table, select **Product2 Quantity** for Feb (cell C6) and drill down to show the detail for this quantity on a fresh worksheet. (You will usually need to double click on the cell).

    This will show us the individual lines of detail which make up the total of 10558 for **Product2** in Feb.

    Your worksheet should look as shown in the image below (possibly with different shading/colours).

	A	B	C	D	E	F	G
1	Products ▾	Quantity ▾	Month ▾	Value ▾			
2	Product2	9583	Feb	14472.7			
3	Product2	975	Feb	416.1			
4							
5							
6							

Sheet5 / Sheet4 / Sheet1 / Sheet2

13. Save your workbook as **T7Exercise3**.

Stage 2

We are going to create a new workbook by copying the data sheet from **T7Exercise3**.

1. With the workbook **T7Exercise3**, select worksheet **Sheet1**, and from the menu, select **Move or Copy Worksheet**.

2. In the **Move or Copy** options, for **To book**, select **New book** from the drop down list of choices. Then select **Create a copy**, so that it is ticked.

3. You will then be presented with a new workbook containing just the sheet of data which we have copied across.

4. Save this new workbook with name **T7Exercise32**.

5.   Switch to the original workbook **T7Exercise3** and you will see that the **Sheet1** with all the data is still present in the workbook. If we had not selected **Create a Copy**, it would have moved to the new workbook, and disappeared from the old workbook.

6.   Select the workbook **T7Exercise32**.

7.   Create a pivot table showing the value of **Product by month**.

8.   Save your spreadsheet (keeping the same name – **T7Exercise32**).

Your spreadsheet should now appear as follows, showing the value of each product by month:

	Sum of Value	Column Labels												
4	Row Labels	Jan	Feb	Mar	Apr	May	Jun	Jul	Aug	Sep	Oct	Nov	Dec	Grand Total
5	Product1	11917.6	41		2222	4100	11273.8	1110.5	191		1500	3884.8	4353.1	40593.8
6	Product2		614.5	14888.8	116		19110.7		11600	3256.3	2579.5	398		7200	2147	61910.8
7	Product3	1646.5	260.8	47628.6	2420			15.131	47285.8	5549.3	23361.5	490		1900	130557.631
8	Product4	600	1147.5	248.64	12086.8	45			4500	11962.9	3386.4	9917.2	562		44456.44
9	Product5		1126	391.1	306	5104.6	62		6200	3600.1	132.5	286.3	213	17421.6
10	Product6	266.9		5400	4800.1	1194.5	542.05	-293		1600	727.5	5089.4	617.9	19945.35
11	Grand Total	15045.5	17464.1	53784.34	21834.9	29554.8	23492.981	55859.6	26482.7	32346	12767.2	17022.5	9231	314885.621

9.   Using the **Drill down** capability, display the detail making up the **Product4** value for **Oct**.

The details should appear as follows:

	A	B	C	D	E
1	Products	Quantity	Month	Value	
2	Product4	27	Oct	600	
3	Product4	13224	Oct	9317.2	
4					

10.   Save your spreadsheet (keeping the same name – **T7Exercise32**)

Exercise 4 – What-If Analysis

In this exercise we are going to practise using the 3 tools within **What-If Analysis**, looking at the outcome of changing values, using **Goal Seek** to find out how to get a specific result, and creating a simple **Data Table**.

Stage 1

1.   Download the spreadsheet **T7WhatIf**.

2.   Open the downloaded file, save the workbook with the new name **T7Exercise4**

3.   The workbook should look as shown below.

	A	B	C	D	E	F	G	H	I
1	Forecast for year								
2		Quarter 1	Quarter 2	Quarter 3	Quarter 4	Total	Assumptions		
3	Sales	£500,000	£525,000	£551,250	£578,813	£2,155,063	5%	(Growth per qtr)	
4	Cost of Sales	£100,000	£105,000	£110,250	£115,763	£431,013	20%	(Perc of Sales)	
5	Gross Profit	£400,000	£420,000	£441,000	£463,050	£1,724,050			
6									
7	Expenses	£125,000	£131,250	£137,813	£144,703	£538,766	25%	(Perc of sales)	
8	Income	£275,000	£288,750	£303,188	£318,347	£1,185,284			

This spreadsheet shows a forecast for Sales and Income based on a number of assumptions, as follows:

.   sales will increase by 5% per qtr (cell G3)

.   cost of sales is 20% of sales value (cell G4)

.   expenses are 25% of sales value (cell G7)

The cells for each quarter are populated with the necessary formulas to use these assumptions and calculate the quarterly values.

We want to consider two scenarios.

The first where we are optimistic and hope that sales will actually be higher and both the cost of sales and expenses lower.

4.   Create a scenario named Optimistic where Sales growth is 10%, cost of sales only 19% of sales, and expenses only 22% of sales. (Note you will need to enter these values as decimals i.e .1, .19, and .22 in the scenario manager)

The second scenario will be poor, with lower sales and higher costs.

5.   Create a scenario named Poor where Sales growth is 2%, cost of sales is 25% of sales, and expenses is 30% of sales. (Again, enter these values as decimals i.e .2, .25, and .3 in the scenario manager)

The scenario manager should now look as shown at the top of the next page.

6. Produce a summary report using these two scenarios, which uses F3, F4, F5, F7 and F8 as the results cells.

The report should look as shown below.

Scenario Summary			
	Current Values:	Optimistic	Poor
Changing Cells:			
$G$3	5%	10%	2%
$G$4	20%	19%	25%
$G$7	25%	22%	30%
Result Cells:			
$F$3	£2,155,063	£2,320,500	£2,060,804
$F$4	£431,013	£440,895	£515,201
$F$5	£1,724,050	£1,879,605	£1,545,603
$F$7	£538,766	£510,510	£618,241
$F$8	£1,185,284	£1,369,095	£927,362

The $F$8 row shows the effect on income of the two different scenarios.

7. Save your workbook as **T7Exercise4**

Stage 2

We are now going to use the **Goal Seek** tool. We want to determine the percentage value we need for cost of sales to allow us to generate a total income of £1,300,000.

1. Open the workbook **T7Exercise4**.

2. Move to worksheet named **Forecast**

3. Select the **Goal Seek** tool

4. Enter the necessary cell reference for the **Set Cell**

5. Enter the required value

6. Specify the **changing** cell

The tool will calculate a solution and display as shown below.

Forecast for year						
	Quarter 1	Quarter 2	Quarter 3	Quarter 4	Total	Assumptions
Sales	£500,000	£525,000	£551,250	£578,813	£2,155,063	5%
Cost of Sales	£73,385	£77,054	£80,907	£84,952	£316,297	15%
Gross Profit	£426,615	£447,946	£470,343	£493,861	£1,838,766	
Expenses	£125,000	£131,250	£137,813	£144,703	£538,766	25%
Income	£301,615	£316,696	£332,531	£349,158	£1,300,000	

Goal Seek Status

Goal Seeking with Cell F8 found a solution.

Step

Pause

Target value: 1300000
Current value: £1,300,000

OK   Cancel

This shows that if the cost of sales could be reduced to 15% of sales, the total income for the year would be £1,300,000.

Stage 3

We are going to create a Data Table to evaluate a series of different growth rates for sales, to determine the effect on total income.

1.   Open the workbook **T7Data Tables**.

The workbook should look as shown below

	A	B	C	D
1	Sales Forecast for Quarter 2			
2		Growth Rate	5%	
3	Sales	Quarter 1	Quarter 2	
4		£500,000	£525,000	
5	Alternative Growth rates	1.0%		
6		1.5%		
7		2.0%		
8		2.5%		
9		3.0%		
10		3.5%		
11		4.0%		
12		4.5%		
13		5.0%		
14		5.5%		
15		6.0%		
16		6.5%		
17		7.0%		
18		7.5%		
19		8.0%		
20		8.5%		
21		9.0%		
22		9.5%		
23		10.0%		

You can see a range of growth rates for sales in the third column. We are going to calculate the possible sales for quarter 2 for each of the growth rates using a Data Table.

2.   Use **Data Tables** to populate the values for Quarter 2

The output should appear as shown on the next page:

◢	A	B	C	D
1	Sales Forecast for Quarter 2			
2		Growth Rate	5%	
3	Sales	Quarter 1	Quarter 2	
4		£500,000	£525,000	
5	Alternative Growth rates	1.0%	£505,000	
6		1.5%	£507,500	
7		2.0%	£510,000	
8		2.5%	£512,500	
9		3.0%	£515,000	
10		3.5%	£517,500	
11		4.0%	£520,000	
12		4.5%	£522,500	
13		5.0%	£525,000	
14		5.5%	£527,500	
15		6.0%	£530,000	
16		6.5%	£532,500	
17		7.0%	£535,000	
18		7.5%	£537,500	
19		8.0%	£540,000	
20		8.5%	£542,500	
21		9.0%	£545,000	
22		9.5%	£547,500	
23		10.0%	£550,000	

3.   Select cell C10

The formula should be as shown in the formula bar below, showing that cell C10 is part of a table based on cell C2.

C10	▼	f_x {=TABLE(,C2)}		
◢	A	B	C	D
1	Sales Forecast for Quarter 2			
2		Growth Rate	5%	
3	Sales	Quarter 1	Quarter 2	
4		£500,000	£525,000	
5	Alternative Growth rates	1.0%	£505,000	
6		1.5%	£507,500	
7		2.0%	£510,000	
8		2.5%	£512,500	
9		3.0%	£515,000	
10		3.5%	£517,500	
11		4.0%	£520,000	

That concludes the exercises for chapter 7.

AAT Sample
Assessment

Sample assessment

This assignment is in one section.

All spreadsheets should be titled and contain a footer with your name, date and AAT registration number.

You are required to open or download an existing spreadsheet. The spreadsheet data is essential and can be downloaded from 'Resources' at www.osbornebooks.co.uk, filename 'AAT Assessment Data'.

The AAT gives candidates two hours 30 minutes (plus 15 minutes reading time) to complete the tasks and a high degree of accuracy is required.

You MUST save your work at regular intervals during this assessment to prevent you losing work.

JA Muddlestone is a wholesaler of surplus stock which they resell to small traders, either via the sales team or over the internet on EBid. You are employed as an accounts clerk in the company. The computer system has crashed and the backup will not load due to a technical problem.

The accountant has asked you to collate some figures into a spreadsheet to give an overview of the activity for the last year.

Over the past year the monthly results have been as follows:

Sales

January	£45,360
February	£53,630
March	£89,340
April	£106,209
May	£119,416
June	£104,197

Expenses

January	£17,262
February	£21,837
March	£23,709
April	£31,286
May	£36,899
June	£36,401

Cost of sales

January	£15,626
February	£18,404
March	£22,416
April	£27,435
May	£31,533
June	£32,189

Task 1

Open a new workbook and save this as 'your initial, surname, date (DD.MM.YY)'

For example JSmith12.12.10SHS.

(a)   Prepare a spreadsheet showing all the figures for sales, expenses and cost of sales. Formulate cells for January to show gross profit and net profit then copy these formulas into the remaining cells for February to June. Gross profit is sales less cost of sales, and net profit is gross profit less expenses. Use formulae to total each column.

(b)   Gross profit margin is calculated as gross profit expressed as a percentage of sales revenue, and net profit margin as net profit expressed as a percentage of sales revenue. Use formulae to calculate these figures for each month, and format the result as a percentage rounded to two decimal places.

(c)   Title this worksheet as 'J A Muddlestone Monthly Figures for 2013' in Arial 10 Bold font in one merged cell centred over the data. Ensure all columns have appropriate headings in bold, and that all totals are displayed in bold font. Save as worksheet 'JAM 1'.

(d)   Copy JAM1 to a new worksheet and display as formula. Save this worksheet as 'JAM1(F)'.

Print out one legible copy of 'JAM1' and 'JAM1(F)', ensuring they each fit on to an A4 page.

Task 2

Open the EBid worksheet.

(a)   Open a new worksheet and copy into it the information from the EBid worksheet. Give the new worksheet the title 'Ebid History' using font size 16, and centre the title on the page. Format headings to bold and ensure column widths and row heights are suitable. Then use the spellcheck function to check and resolve any errors.

(b)   Insert a row between books and collectables, input 'coins' in column 'Auction Type', and '1910 SHILLING' in column 'Item'. Input bids 1 to 12 of £4, £31, £65, £84, £198, £175, £205, £265, £320, £289, £400 and £432, respectively.

(c)   Insert two new columns between columns B and C using the column headings 'AVERAGE' and 'MEDIAN'. Use appropriate functions to calculate these for each of the items listed.

(d)   Change the format of all numerical cells to currency rounded to the nearest £. Use conditional formatting to change cell content to red for the highest bid for each item on the worksheet.

(e)   Produce a line chart to show the bid history of JP computers. Insert the line chart below the bid figures, ensuring it is appropriately labelled and has a suitable title. Save worksheet as 'E-BID' and print, ensuring the data and graph will fit on a sheet of A4 paper.

Task 3

Parkins Motors are a large car dealership, selling a range of luxury cars and accessories.

(a) Open the sales commission data for Parkins Cars – there are two worksheets for this, 'Salesforce results' and 'Parkins % commission rates'.

Copy and paste the data from the Parkins salesforce worksheet into a new worksheet, then use this and the data in the 'Parkins % commission rates' worksheet. Insert formulae to calculate:

1.   the total value of all sales revenue

2.   the commission earned by each sales person on each make of car (to two decimal places)

3.   the total of sales revenue earned by each sales person

4.   the total commissions earned by each sales person

5.   the total value of sales revenue for each make of car

6.   the total value of commission for each make of car.

(b) Format the spreadsheet with:

· titles in bold

· currency figures to two decimal places

· column width adjusted as necessary, so that all figures and headings are visible.

(c) Sort the spreadsheet alphabetically by family name order. Save the worksheet with the name 'Parkinsalphalist'.

(d) Copy the information from 'Parkinsalphalist' to a new worksheet. On the new worksheet, use a function to calculate the average value of total sales per sales person, clearly identifying this.

(e) If any salesperson has total sales of more than 20% above the average value for sales made by all the sales force, then a bonus of 0.5% of their individual total sales figure should be given. Head a column 'BONUS', use an 'IF' statement to calculate this bonus, and then total all bonuses to be paid.

(f) Insert a column to the left of all data and head this 'RANK'. Then rank the spreadsheet by total sales value, from the highest to the lowest value. Display the results in ranked descending order of sales value. Save as worksheet with file name 'Parkinsranked'. Print this worksheet.

Task 4

Parkins Motors also sell a range of car accessories. These are sold across the country in showrooms, across the internet and from their own catalogue.

(a) Open the 'accessories' worksheet and copy this data to a new worksheet. Create two pivot tables: one to show the total sales revenue from the different ways the goods were sold, and one to show the total sales revenue from each city in column B.

The pivot tables should be displayed to the right of the data provided, one under the other. Save this, naming the worksheet as 'Pivots'. Fill the cells yellow to show the city and the amount with the highest sales revenue, and the type of sale and amount that has the highest sales revenue.

Task 5

Short answer questions

Note: Candidates must tick a box to indicate their answer for each Task 5 question.

(a) If you wanted to annotate the data in a pie chart, what would you do?

✓

Name the axes.	
Use a legend.	
Write an explanation next to the chart.	
Give the chart a title.	

(b) What would you use the PMT function for?

✓

Calculate the interest rate if you know the term and monthly payments of a loan.	
Calculate the term when you know the principal and interest rate of a loan.	
Calculate the payment if you have the principal, interest rate and term of a loan.	
Do a permanent memory transfer of data across workbooks.	

(c)   What does the error message '#REF!' mean?

✓

You have used a function instead of a formula.	
The formula you have entered is invalid.	
There is a problem with the cell reference.	
You have made an error with a mathematical sign.	

(d)   You require users to amend figures within a worksheet, but you also wish to prevent people writing in a number of key cells. What would you do?

✓

Hide the cells.	
Protect the cells.	
Use conditional formatting.	
Ask them not to alter anything on the worksheet.	

(e)   You need to use the Euro sign on a worksheet. What do you do?

✓

You cannot do this as it is not on the keyboard.	
Use an E as a recognised abbreviation.	
Format the cell as currency, and then select 'Euro'.	
Write 'Euro' as a heading to the column.	

Assessment
answers

Task 1

JAM1 printout

J A Muddlestone Monthly figures for 2013

Month	Sales Income	Cost of goods sold	Gross Profit	Expenses	Profit for the period	Gross Profit Margin	Net Profit Margin %
Jan	45,360	15,626	29,734	17,262	12,472	65.55%	27.50%
Feb	53,630	18,404	35,226	21,837	13,389	65.68%	24.97%
Mar	89,340	22,416	66,924	23,709	43,215	74.91%	48.37%
Apr	106,209	27,435	78,774	31,286	47,488	74.17%	44.71%
May	119,416	31,533	87,883	36,899	50,984	73.59%	42.69%
June	104,197	32,189	72,008	36,401	35,607	69.11%	34.17%
Totals	518,152	147,603	370,549	167,394	203,155		

JAM1(F) printout

J A Muddlestone Monthly figures for 2013

Month	Sales Income	Cost of goods sold	Gross Profit	Expenses	Profit for the period	Gross Profit Margin	Net Profit Margin %
Jan	45360	15626	=B4-C4	17262	=D4-E4	=D4/B4	=F4/B4
Feb	53630	18404	=B5-C5	21837	=D5-E5	=D5/B5	=F5/B5
Mar	89340	22416	=B6-C6	23709	=D6-E6	=D6/B6	=F6/B6
Apr	106209	27435	=B7-C7	31286	=D7-E7	=D7/B7	=F7/B7
May	119416	31533	=B8-C8	36899	=D8-E8	=D8/B8	=F8/B8
June	104197	32189	=B9-C9	36401	=D9-E9	=D9/B9	=F9/B9
Totals	=SUM(B4:B9)	=SUM(C4:C9)	=SUM(D4:D9)	=SUM(E4:E9)	=SUM(F4:F9)		

Task 2

E-BID printout

Ebid History

AUCTION TYPE	ITEM	AVERAGE	MEDIAN	BID 1	BID 2	BID 3	BID 4	BID 5	BID 6	BID 7	BID 8	BID 9	BID 10	BID 11	BID 12
electronics	100 JP COMPUTERS	£6,065	£6,258	£2,345	£3,500	£3,675	£4,000	£5,720	£6,795	£8,200	£9,950	£7,540	£4,250	£9,360	£7,450
art & music	SIGNED BEATLES SHE LOVES YOU	£2,563	£2,695	£1,000	£1,250	£4,230	£2,100	£3,000	£3,150	£3,350	£3,500	£1,475	£1,545	£2,390	£3,765
Fashion	50 MARY QUANT DRESSES	£4,326	£4,429	£2,500	£1,225	£2,975	£3,500	£6,230	£4,707	£5,575	£6,375	£5,975	£4,150	£2,250	£6,450
books	10 SIGNED HARRY POTTER 1ST EDITION	£110,523	£70,325	£12,500	£25,500	£75,750	£55,555	£64,900	£42,575	£92,400	£635,000	£37,500	£105,000	£79,599	£99,999
coins	1910 SHILLING	£206	£202	£4	£31	£65	£84	£198	£175	£205	£265	£320	£289	£400	£432
collectables	LIMITED EDITION FIGURINE OF DANCER	£842	£1,001	£25	£50	£100	£1,295	£950	£1,000	£1,425	£1,100	£575	£1,001	£1,150	£1,430
electronics	500 XBOX SYSTEM	£5,718	£5,538	£4,400	£4,550	£4,700	£4,275	£5,400	£7,430	£6,900	£7,200	£5,760	£4,900	£7,425	£5,675
games	500 MARIO GAMES	£350	£348	£10	£125	£75	£350	£225	£345	£475	£700	£424	£90	£675	£701

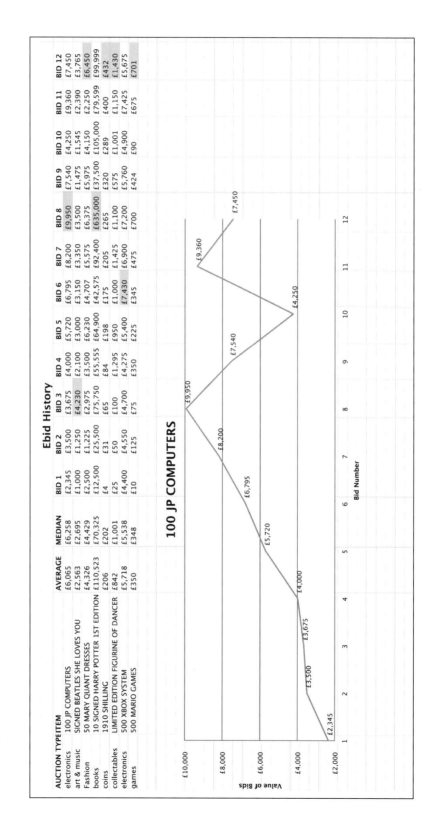

100 JP COMPUTERS

Value of Bids / Bid Number

Task 3

Parkinsalphalist printout

FAMILY NAME	FIRST NAME	TOYOTA Sales	TOYOTA Commission	HONDA Sales	HONDA Commission	FORD Sales	FORD Commission	TOTALS Sales	TOTALS Commission
BINNS	STANLEY	£21,432.00	£642.96	£74,324.00	£3,716.20	£17,689.00	£1,326.68	£113,445.00	£5,685.84
BLACK	JANET	£32,678.00	£980.34	£53,535.00	£2,676.75	£68,231.00	£5,117.33	£154,444.00	£8,774.42
IDAWO	BERNARD	£42,762.00	£1,282.86	£42,245.00	£2,112.25	£29,872.00	£2,240.40	£114,879.00	£5,635.51
LINDO-UNAN	GEORGE	£48,735.00	£1,462.05	£72,623.00	£3,631.15	£97,532.00	£7,314.90	£218,890.00	£12,408.10
SMITH	LYNN	£50,950.00	£1,528.50	£53,345.00	£2,667.25	£76,799.00	£5,759.93	£181,094.00	£9,955.68
STEVENSON	PAUL	£36,758.00	£1,102.74	£53,572.00	£2,678.60	£19,022.00	£1,426.65	£109,352.00	£5,207.99
	Totals	£233,315.00	£6,999.45	£349,644.00	£17,482.20	£309,145.00	£23,185.88	£892,104.00	£47,667.53

Parkinsranked printout

RANK	FAMILY NAME	FIRST NAME	TOYOTA Sales	TOYOTA Commission	HONDA Sales	HONDA Commission	FORD Sales	FORD Commission	TOTALS Sales	TOTALS Commission	Bonus
1	LINDO-UNAN	GEORGE	£48,735.00	£1,462.05	£72,623.00	£3,631.15	£97,532.00	£7,314.90	£218,890.00	£12,408.10	£1,094.45
2	SMITH	LYNN	£50,950.00	£1,528.50	£53,345.00	£2,667.25	£76,799.00	£5,759.93	£181,094.00	£9,955.68	£905.47
3	BLACK	JANET	£32,678.00	£980.34	£53,535.00	£2,676.75	£68,231.00	£5,117.33	£154,444.00	£8,774.42	£0.00
4	IDAWO	BERNARD	£42,762.00	£1,282.86	£42,245.00	£2,112.25	£29,872.00	£2,240.40	£114,879.00	£5,635.51	£0.00
5	BINNS	STANLEY	£21,432.00	£642.96	£74,324.00	£3,716.20	£17,689.00	£1,326.68	£113,445.00	£5,685.84	£0.00
6	STEVENSON	PAUL	£36,758.00	£1,102.74	£53,572.00	£2,678.60	£19,022.00	£1,426.65	£109,352.00	£5,207.99	£0.00
		Totals	£233,315.00	£6,999.45	£349,644.00	£17,482.20	£309,145.00	£23,185.88	£892,104.00	£47,667.53	£1,999.92
		Average							£148,684.00		

Task 4

ACCESSORIES SALES

Transid	WHERE	WHAT	HOW	REVENUE
1	Leeds	air freshener	Store	80
2	London	GPS system	catalogue	1794
3	Birmingham	wiper blades	Store	16
4	London	Reversing guides	Store	885
5	Hull	Bluetooth manual	Store	165
6	Edinburgh	MP3 player	Store	1196
7	Glasgow	Reversing guides	Store	590
8	London	Reversing guides	Store	1475
9	Cardiff	Bluetooth manual	Store	165
10	London	GPS system	catalogue	2392
11	London	Boot tidy	Store	190
12	Hull	Reversing guides	Store	590
13	London	air coolants	Store	130
14	London	wiper blades	catalogue	40
15	Glasgow	Map case	Store	75
16	Hull	Reversing guides	catalogue	590
17	London	Bluetooth manual	Store	220
18	Leeds	reversing camera	Store	1056
19	Birmingham	GPS system	catalogue	1196
20	London	Bluetooth manual	Web	275
21	Edinburgh	reversing camera	catalogue	1760
22	Glasgow	cup holder	Store	102
23	London	air coolants	catalogue	104
24	Glasgow	Bluetooth manual	catalogue	275
25	Hull	wiper blades	Store	32
26	Edinburgh	Reversing guides	Store	1180
27	Glasgow	MP3 player	Store	1196
28	London	wiper blades	Web	16
29	Hull	wiper blades	Store	24
30	London	Bluetooth manual	Store	165
31	London	air freshener	Store	40
32	London	Reversing guides	Store	295
33	London	MP3 player	catalogue	2392
34	London	CD player	Store	1056
35	Leeds	wiper blades	Store	16
36	Leeds	air freshener	Store	60
37	Edinburgh	air freshener	catalogue	40
38	Leeds	Bluetooth manual	Web	220
39	London	cup holder	Store	34
40	Glasgow	wiper blades	Store	40
41	Glasgow	Bluetooth manual	Store	220
42	Hull	Map case	Store	30
43	Leeds	air freshener	Store	20
44	Edinburgh	cup holder	Web	34
45	Birmingham	air coolants	Store	52
46	London	Bluetooth manual	Store	110
47	London	cup holder	Store	34
48	Birmingham	MP3 player	Store	1196
49	London	MP3 player	Store	1196
50	Glasgow	cup holder	catalogue	170
51	London	CD player	catalogue	704
52	Birmingham	air coolants	Store	130
53	Edinburgh	Boot tidy	Store	475

Sum of REVENUE

HOW	Total
catalogue	11457
Store	14536
Web	545
Grand Total	26538

Sum of REVENUE

WHERE	Total
Birmingham	2590
Cardiff	165
Edinburgh	4685
Glasgow	2668
Hull	1431
Leeds	1452
London	13547
Grand Total	26538

Task 5

(a) Use a legend.

(b) Calculate the payment if you have the principal, interest rate and term of a loan.

(c) There is a problem with the cell reference.

(d) Protect the cell.

(e) Format the cell as currency, and then select 'Euro'.

Index

for your notes

for your notes